THE BIG BRITISH RAILWAY JOURNEYS PUZZLE BOOK

THE BIG BRITISH RAILWAY JOURNEYS PUZZLE BOOK

Travel across the country in over 100 mind-boggling puzzles

National Railway Museum
with Roy & Sue Preston

SEVEN
DIALS

First published in Great Britain in 2021 by Seven Dials
an imprint of The Orion Publishing Group Ltd
Carmelite House, 50 Victoria Embankment
London EC4Y 0DZ

An Hachette UK Company

1 3 5 7 9 10 8 6 4 2

Text © SCMG Enterprises Ltd 2021
Puzzles © The Orion Publishing Group Ltd 2021
Puzzles written by Roy & Sue Preston

A CIP catalogue record for this book is
available from the British Library.

ISBN (Trade paperback) 978 1 8418 8561 2
ISBN (eBook) 978 1 8418 8562 9

Designed by us-now.com
Printed and bound in Great Britain by Clays Ltd, Elcograf, S.p.A

MIX
Paper from
responsible sources
FSC
www.fsc.org   FSC® C104740

www.orionbooks.co.uk

CONTENTS

Section One

THE GREATEST CHALLENGE

THE GREATEST CHALLENGE

Travelling by train is unique. In a car, you take the strain of driving yourself, and even if you are lucky enough to have someone to do that for you, you are still jolted around by potholes, twisting roads and traffic lights. Not to mention the ubiquitous traffic jam. In a plane, you are sealed in a tube, packed tightly with fellow passengers, perhaps with the tiniest porthole to view a distant world. On the open seas, there is simply nothing to see. Yet board a train, and you can sit back, relax and enjoy a close-up view of the world as you pass it by. Only on a train does the journey truly become the *raison d'être* to travel. Indeed, across Britain and the world, many people do travel by train just for the sake of it. From heritage railways to long-distance land cruises, sometimes never leaving a station, the train is the experience.

Of course not all journeys by train are created equal. Open fields and urban architecture can have their own beauty but peruse any curated list of the most beautiful railway journeys (there are many) and they will all share one thing in common: a spectacular view of some of the world's most breathtaking landscapes. From mountains, hills and glaciers, to valleys, rivers and deserts, the most popular railway journeys frequently traverse the most varied and magnificent environments.

However, the landscapes that elevate the beauty of these railways also presented the greatest challenges to the engineers and builders tasked with constructing them. Railways do not like hills. A steel wheel on a steel rail has many advantages compared to a rubber tyre on a road, but adhesion (the friction that prevents the wheel from slipping) is not one of them. That means that railways must be as flat and straight as possible, hence why mountains and valleys present such a tall challenge. Yet, thankfully, railway engineers were more than prepared to conquer them.

The Forth Bridge

As the railways came to Scotland in the nineteenth century, the broad estuaries of the Forth and Tay rivers posed a huge obstacle to engineers trying to link Edinburgh to north-east Scotland. Initially, they simply went around them but the diversion around the Firth of Forth added around 50 miles and more than an hour to the journey. A train ferry across the Forth helped to cut journey times a little, but ultimately bridges across the estuaries proved a far better solution. In the 1870s, engineer Thomas Bouch therefore designed two bridges for the crossings. The first to be completed was the Tay Bridge in 1878, but in late 1879 the bridge collapsed in a storm, plunging a train and around seventy-five people to their deaths. Bouch carried the blame for the disaster and construction of his Forth Bridge was halted.

In response, the new engineers appointed to build the bridge devised one of the world's most iconic engineering wonders. Opened on 4 March 1890, Sir John Fowler and Sir Benjamin Baker's cantilever bridge is a classic of Victorian over-engineering. Modern-day understanding of material sciences allows twenty-first-century engineers to work within fine tolerances to produce sleek and elegant designs that save on materials. However, prior to this technical knowledge, the solution to ensuring no repeat of the Tay Bridge disaster was to spare no expense in building the strongest structure possible. The Forth Bridge was therefore the first major structure in Britain to be built entirely from steel. It used 53,000 tons of the metal, plus 92,000 cubic metres of concrete and some six and a half million rivets to bridge the 2.5 kilometre distance over the Forth. Engineers now believe the bridge is so strong it will survive well beyond the next century.

The navvies of the Settle to Carlisle Railway

Despite famous engineers usually taking the credit for the construction of railways, they were not actually the men who built them. In Britain, that job fell to the navvies, whose name derived from the navigators that dug the canals of the eighteenth century. Their job was tough. They dug and built tunnels, cuttings, embankments and bridges by hand. Their lives were constantly on the move as they followed the construction on the railway across the landscape. They only settled into longer-term camps when the advance of railway slowed at the sites of tunnels and viaducts.

While navvies had a reputation for drunkenness, violence and crime, the reality was more nuanced. For example, missionaries and church ministers held open-air services on Sundays, attended by the workers and their families who camped with them. Many of the navvies were also Irish immigrants and were victim to racism and prejudice. The communities developed their own culture in which folk songs (and drinking) played an important part. Death and injury were also an everyday part of life, as were diseases like smallpox and cholera in the poor conditions of the camps. They were also frequently underpaid when the costs of projects overran. So, while their behaviour was sometimes questionable, their actions were being made within some dire circumstances.

The Settle to Carlisle line, built for the Midland Railway, was the last main-line railway to be built mostly by hand by railway navvies, and it was also one of the most gruelling. Its summit at Ais Gill is the highest in England and the railway included fourteen tunnels and twenty-two viaducts. The line took seven years to construct, and work was often paused due to frozen ground, snowdrifts or flooding. It took 6000 men around seven years to construct the railway. The death toll was not recorded, but as an example, it is known that eighty died in a single smallpox outbreak at one camp.

Although it was threatened with closure in the 1980s, the railway survived thanks to local campaigners. Today, it is among the most popular in Britain.

It draws tourists from around the world and the surrounding hills are one of the most popular rambling destinations in England. At the heart of the line is the twenty-four-arch Ribblehead Viaduct. It is an attraction in its own right, and a popular destination for photographers.

Railways in the extreme

Not every engineer can employ every resource available to flatten their railways with tunnels and viaducts though. Engineers sometimes ignored the problem and sought alternative solutions. Nineteenth-century passengers on the Liverpool and Manchester Railway began their journeys from Liverpool on trains hauled not by locomotives but by ropes powered by stationary steam engines that dragged their trains up the hill to Edge Hill. That was not the most practical solution though.

The limit for the steepest possible railway is hard to define, but as the gradient increases, trains slow down. This can be combated with more powerful engines, or by reducing the weight of the train, but that makes the trains more expensive to run and less productive. The two-miles-long Lickey Incline in Worcestershire is the steepest main-line railway in Britain at 1 in 37 (it climbs 1 metre in elevation for every 37 metres distance) and is the only section of British railway to still make frequent use of dedicated banking engines to push freight trains up the hill.

Another solution was simply to reduce the width of the track. Smaller trains on narrower tracks required smaller tunnels, bridges, cuttings and embankments and could negotiate tighter corners, making them far easier and cheaper to build. Such narrow-gauge railways had been used in mines and industry for centuries, using horses to pull the wagons. However, in the 1860s the Ffestiniog Railway Company in north-west Wales proved that steam locomotives could be adapted to the purpose as well, becoming the world's first steam-hauled narrow-gauge passenger railway. Today it is the world's oldest working railway company and offers a spectacular journey from the historic slate mining town of Blaenau Ffestiniog to the coastal town of Porthmadog. Following on from Ffestiniog's success, narrow-gauge railways could be found in mountainous regions around the world, perhaps most notably in the foothills of the Himalayas on the Darjeeling and Shimla railways.

Sometimes, though, no amount of tunnelling and earthworks will solve the problem. However, there is one last solution for railway engineers: the rack railway. These railways still used rails to guide the train, but to allow the engine to pull the train up the hill, the engine uses a pinion (a cogwheel) with teeth that insert into a rack (a slotted rail) between the tracks. The first such mountain railway was built to take tourists to the top of Mount Washington in New Hampshire, USA, but the country that truly took the technology to heart was Switzerland. Among the peaks of the Alps, passengers can enjoy the scenery from more than twenty rack railways that link mountain towns and transport tourists and skiers. Switzerland is also home to the world's steepest rack railway – the Pilatus Railway with a gradient of 1 in 2.1 and climbs 1.6 kilometres from Lake Lucerne to the peaks of Mount Pilatus. Closer to home, the Snowdon Mountain Railway uses the rack system to take tourists on a journey to the peak of Wales's tallest mountain to offer them panoramic views of Snowdonia.

1. COGNITIVE

The cogs in the wheel all have SIX letters. Solve the railway-linked clues below. Some answers are written clockwise and some anti-clockwise – it's up to you to work out which is the correct way. The first letter of Answer 1 is in place.

1 Nails or bolts for securing metal plates

2 Reach your destination

3 They assist the stopping of the locomotive

4 Travel voucher

5 Competing at speed

6 Sets off, begins

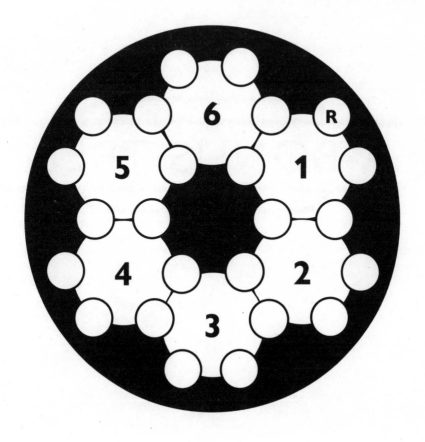

2. STATIONGRAM

Rearrange the letters to spell out the name of a station.

3. A LONG DAY

The work of a navvy was physically demanding. The hours could be long and he could be moved around a number of different jobs.

- On one day a worker started at 7.00 a.m.

- He spent a quarter of his working day using a pickaxe.

- He spent 35 per cent of his time loading wagons.

- He spent five hours digging.

- The traditional call of 'Yo-ho, Yo-ho!' signalled the end of the shift.

- What time was that?

4. A TO Z

This puzzle looks like an ordinary crossword. However, there are no clues. The letters A to Z are each represented by a number instead. We have given you the numbers that represent the letters in the word **SPEED** to start you off. All the answers in the crossword grid have a railway link.

The checklist below will help you to keep track of the letters you have found.

1 = **S**, 2 = **P**, 3 = **E**, 4 = **D**,

5 = , 6 = , 7 = , 8 = , 9 = , 10 = , 11 = , 12 = , 13 = , 14 = , 15 = , 16 = , 17 = , 18 = , 19 = , 20 = , 21 = , 22 = , 23 = , 24, = , 25 = , 26 = .

	14		15		12				21		15		25	
4	3	7	6	5	8		11	2	3	7	6	14	11	7
	6		16		6				23		7		19	
6	7	3	6		1	2	3	3	4		21	11	6	14
	11		7		1		9				11		13	
8	11	6	4	1		1	12	15	3	4	26	8	3	1
	10		1		6		26		6		7			
	1		3	9	2	7	3	1	1			12		
		17		8		1		14		12		11		
12	6	22	3	14	3	7	5	6		20	11	5	23	1
	8		3				11		14		23		14	
8	5	23	18		10	11	23	3	19		14	26	7	23
	13		3		6				7		11		11	
12	15	6	23	13	5	23	13		3	24	26	6	8	1
	14		4		8				1		7		1	

5. CHANGING STATIONS

Each wheel contains six individual letters. Two letters are shared with the other wheels. One question mark sign, which indicates a letter common to all three words, appears in the centre. Decide on the mystery letter, then use the letters to make three railway stations with **NINE** letters in each.

Set the wheels in motion and begin the journey, which will take you to the North West of England.

1 _ _ _ _ _ _ _ _

2 _ _ _ _ _ _ _ _ _

3 _ _ _ _ _ _ _ _ _

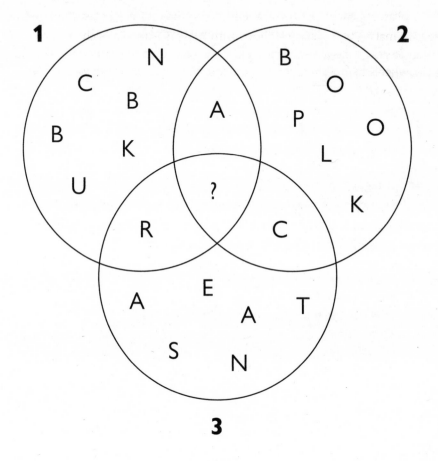

6. PASS TIMES

A single track, narrow gauge rack railway runs up into the Alps in Switzerland.

There are five stations on the line with a loop section of track allowing the train to turn around at each station. It is exactly 8 miles from the lowest station to reach the highest station and have the train in position for the downward return.

The gradient is very steep and there are strict speed limits in place. The train travels at 10 miles per hour when climbing up the mountain. It travels at 15 miles per hour when making the downward trip.

The first trip goes to the top of the line. The train then makes the descent down the line. On the next trip the train ascends half the length of the previous journey and then returns. This pattern of halving the length of the previous journey is repeated with each following trip.

How far has the train travelled in total?

For how long has the train been moving along the track?

Brunel's Birthday

If you catch a train from Bath to London, one of the first landmarks you encounter is Box Tunnel. Part of Isambard Kingdom Brunel's Great Western Railway, it was the longest railway tunnel in the world when it opened in 1841. One often rumoured peculiarity is that on Brunel's birthday (9 April) the sun would shine straight down the length of the tunnel. It is certainly a compelling story. It speaks to the grandeur and excess that we associate with Victorian engineers and our own sense of playfulness. Surely, we would do the same if we were in Brunel's position? Unfortunately, it is not true. The sun does shine through the tunnel, but only on 6 April, three days before Brunel's birthday. When the railway was closed on a sunny 9 April morning in 2017, engineers checked and although the wet tunnel walls did reflect the sun some distance into the tunnel (perhaps how the rumours began) it did not shine down its length. Should Brunel truly have wanted to make the alignment, he would both have had access to the necessary astronomical information in the 1830s and the means to adjust the alignment accordingly. So, it seems unlikely that the story is anything more than a coincidence.

7. PUZZLE TRIP

Who could have guessed in the early days of rail travel how this means of transport would change people's lives and enrich them? Taking the train gives you the option of simply drinking in the fabulous scenery or exercising the brain by reading, writing or doing puzzles. What could be better?

The successful challenge of bringing the railways to Scotland really opened up this beautiful landscape with the building of the Tay Bridge and the Forth Bridge. Each of our five twenty-first-century travellers is enjoying a trip by train north of Edinburgh. Each person travels to a different destination and has solved a different number of puzzles on the journey. Each one has a favourite puzzle type.

Use the information below so that you can fill in the upper grid. When you find a piece of positive information put a tick in the correct box. Put a cross when you have found a piece of negative information. Cross-refer until you can complete the box at the foot of the page.

1 Mr Winner, on his way to Gleneagles loves tackling a sudoku.

2 The person heading for Inverness solves four puzzles. Neither she nor the other lady like logic problems.

3 Mr Down, a crossword fanatic, solves five puzzles on the trip.

4 The word fit expert completes one puzzle more than the traveller heading for Aviemore, who in turn does one puzzle more than Ms Smart.

5 A gentleman was en route to Stirling.

	Destination					Puzzles Solved					Puzzle Type				
	Aviemore	Gleneagles	Inverness	Kingussie	Stirling	One	Two	Three	Four	Five	Crosswords	Logic	Sudoku	Word fit	Word search
Name															
Mr Bright															
Mrs Cross															
Mr Down															
Ms Smart															
Mr Winner															
Puzzle Type															
Crosswords															
Logic															
Sudoku															
Word fit															
Word search															
Puzzles Solved															
One															
Two															
Three															
Four															
Five															

Name	Destination	Puzzles Solved	Puzzle Type

8. MAKING TRACKS

You have to lay down the tracks within the grid, starting in the bottom left grid as indicated. The railway exits in the bottom right grid.

There are six types of track that can be used:

- Straight section of track running **North** to **South**.

- Straight section of track running **East** to **West**.

- Section of track that curves – there are **four** options for these.

The areas showing mountain peaks cannot be crossed by rail tracks.

One piece of track is already in place.

The pieces of track used in section A are:
1 x **East West**; 4 x **Curved**.

The pieces of track used in section B are:
3 x **North South**; 2 x **Curved**.

The pieces of track used in section C are:
1 x **North South**; 4 x **Curved**.

The pieces of track used in section D are:
1 x **North South**; 2 x **East West**; 2 x **Curved**.

The pieces of track used in section E are:
1 x **North South**; 2 x **Curved**.

The pieces of track used in section F are:
2 x **East West**; 2 x **Curved**.

Can you complete the plan to lay the tracks?

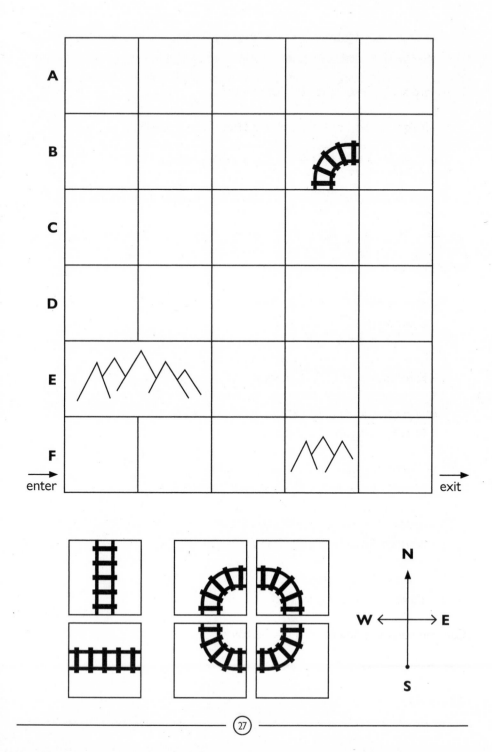

9. LINE NINE

Each number from 1 to 9 represents a different letter of the alphabet. Solve the clues and write the letters in the appropriate spaces in the grid. When all nine letters are in place a famous railway landmark is created. It is made up of two words.

1	2	3	4	5	6	7	8	9

Clues

A Gate or obstacle blocking access   4255695

B Prepared, raring to go   59273

C G stands for this in GWR   85921

Stations

Our railway journeys always begin and end at stations, but how well do you know them?

1 Which is Britain's busiest station?

2 Which station is Britain's busiest outside London?

3 What do Llantisilly, Knapford, Felpersham and Snettleford stations have in common?

4 Sorted alphabetically, which is Britain's first station?

5 And last station?

6 What is the longest station name in Britain?

7 Name three British stations with three-letter names.

8 Which was Britain's least used station in 2019/20?

9 Where is Britain's longest station bench?

10. FROM A RAILWAY CARRIAGE

Here is a memorable poem by Robert Louis Stevenson written in 1885. The rhythm of the poem echoes the rhythm of a railway train as it travels at increasing speeds. The thirty-one words in capital letters can all be found in the letter grid. They are all in straight lines and can go across, backwards, up, down or diagonally. There is one word from the poem that appears twice in the word search. Which is it?

'From a **Railway Carriage**' *by Robert Louis Stevenson*

Faster than **FAIRIES**, faster than **WITCHES**,
BRIDGES and **HOUSES**, **HEDGES** and **DITCHES**;
And charging along like **TROOPS** in a **BATTLE**,
All through the **MEADOWS** the **HORSES** and **CATTLE**:
All of the **SIGHTS** of the **HILL** and the **PLAIN**
Fly as thick as driving **RAIN**;
And ever again, in the wink of an **EYE**,
Painted **STATIONS** whistle by.
Here is a **CHILD** who clambers and scrambles,
All by himself and gathering **BRAMBLES**;
Here is a **TRAMP** who stands and gazes;
And there is the **GREEN** for stringing the **DAISIES**.
And here is a **CART** run away in the **ROAD**
Lumping along with **MAN** and **LOAD**;
And here is a **MILL** and there is a **RIVER**:
Each a **GLIMPSE** and gone for ever!

```
F  J  C  Z  T  E  C  C  T  N  B  X  R  L  H
L  A  H  P  N  E  N  A  E  A  E  M  Z  L  O
U  S  I  G  H  T  S  E  T  R  S  E  H  T  R
B  G  L  R  Y  O  R  T  O  T  S  I  Q  U  S
R  H  D  Z  I  G  L  A  I  P  L  A  I  N  E
A  C  A  R  T  E  D  O  M  L  S  E  T  L  S
M  E  A  D  O  W  S  I  A  P  K  L  R  T  E
B  A  J  I  X  E  L  H  T  D  R  E  A  L  S
L  O  N  T  H  G  Y  R  D  Y  V  T  S  E  S
E  J  R  C  L  O  O  E  A  I  I  E  I  W  E
S  L  T  H  R  O  U  W  R  O  G  S  E  L  G
T  I  G  E  P  M  L  S  N  D  I  O  L  I  D
W  U  L  S  P  I  J  S  E  A  B  I  C  G  I
A  E  O  Y  A  L  S  H  D  S  M  N  I  A  R
C  A  R  R  I  A  G  E  S  E  G  D  I  R  B
```

11. RACK RAILWAYS

In this puzzle, letters have been replaced by shapes. The code is constant for all the groups. Each group names a country where a rack railway has been developed.

The first group of shapes reveals the country where the Ffestiniog Railway Company was founded. (Forgotten the name? The info appears in this section.) When you have cracked the code for the first group, there are FIVE letters that you can place in the second group and that should set you on your way to naming the country.

What do the other groups stand for?

1 ✺ ✡ ✪ ✛ ✱

2 ✳ ✺ ☆ ✳ ✺ ✛ ✲ ✪ ✡ ✪ ♣

3 ☆ ✪ ♣ ☆ ✡

4 ✛ ✲ ✡ ✺ ☆ ✪

5 ☆ ✳ ✡ ✪ ✺

6 ✳ ✩ ✡ ☆ ✪

12. STATIONGRAM

Rearrange the letters to spell out the name of a station.

13. MAP THE JOURNEY

The eight railway stations have had the letters in their names arranged in alphabetical order. Unravel the names and match them to the numbers on the map to identify four famous railway journeys. We give you a list of four journey distances. Can you match them to the journeys? Happy travelling!

ABDEEENR

ACEENNPZ

AFIILLMORTW (two words)

AGGLOSW

AGHIMNNOTT

DINNOSW

DDEENU

EEGKNSSS

Distances	Journeys
58 miles	1 to 2
63 miles	3 to 4
123 miles	5 to 6
191 miles	7 to 8

14. WHERE AM I?

Use the riddles to work out the letters that name the station at the end of the journey.

My first is in **START**
And also in **STOP**.

My second is in **TOURS**
But isn't in **SHOP**.

My third is in **HAUL**
But isn't in **HALL**.

My fourth is in **CAR**
But isn't in **CALL**.

My fifth is in **COAST**
But isn't in **CAST**.

It's the end of my journey.
I've arrived here at last!

London's Other Underground

Railways are built in tunnels to avoid following the steep gradients of mountainous terrain, but there are other obstacles on the surface that railway engineers like to avoid. That is most obvious in cities like London, where building new railways above ground involves buying and then demolishing a vast number of homes and businesses. London was the world's first city to build an underground passenger railway (the Metropolitan) but passengers are not the only things moved by rail underneath London. The Post Office built an underground railway to carry mail between nine sorting offices through London between Whitechapel and Paddington. It operated from 1927 to 2003 and tourists can now ride on a short section of the railway. London's strangest underground railway is a more recent addition. In the early 2000s a tunnel was built from Elstree to St John's Wood to carry high voltage electrical cables. Just like overhead cables, they require frequent inspection, but it would be far too dangerous for engineers to walk through the 12-mile tunnel. The tunnel therefore includes a suspended monorail, which can autonomously inspect the cables or safely carry engineers to the site of a fault.

15. SLANGING MATCH

The navvies who built the railways developed their own slang, not unlike Cockney rhyming slang. They would know what the words were referring to but 'outsiders' would not. Here are some examples. In each case, can you have a stab at working out the word that is represented by the slang? Undoubtedly, there are many examples when it's best not to know what the rhymes stand for, but these are all in the best of taste!

All the matching words can be found in the letter square. Words are all in straight lines and can go across, backwards, up, down or diagonally.

1 LORD LOVEL

2 BARK AND GROWL

3 SUGAR AND HONEY

4 FROG AND TOAD

5 BILLY GORMAN

6 PIG'S EAR

7 JIMMY SKINNER

8 TIDDLY WINK

```
F   R   W   I   Y   T   D
S   O   D   A   E   B   I
H   F   R   A   N   E   N
O   C   I   E   O   E   N
V   M   N   D   M   R   E
E   R   K   O   U   A   R
L   E   W   O   R   T   N
```

16. QUOTABILITY

Solve the clues and put your answers in the correct squares in the grid. All the answers have EIGHT letters. When the upper grid is complete the first column reading down will reveal the name of an author who had very firm views about the railways. Transfer the keycoded letters to the lower grid and complete a quotation by him, which begins: 'I am never sure of time or place upon a railroad.'

1   A chart of days and dates, relevant to railway timetables

2   Vacations, periods of time away from work

3   Went forward, progressed

4   Illumination which tells you to go no further (3,5)

5   Person who carries out manual work

6   Go abroad to live, as those who left Liverpool often did in the nineteenth century

7   Ticket which is not first, second or third class

8   Journeys that didn't involve an overnight stay (3,5)

9   Slopes, gentle hills

10 Railway carriage passage that leads to compartments

11 Precious memento brought back as a reminder of a visit

12 Technician, person in charge of machines

13 Complex railway systems

14 Coming to a halt

	A	B	C	D	E	F	G	H
1								
2								
3								
4								
5								
6								
7								
8								
9								
10								
11								
12								
13								
14								

D2	■	F3	B5	D7	,	D8	■	C10	B11	B1	C4	■	C6
	■				,		■					■	
C9	F2	E12	,	C13	■	B14	G4	F8	G14	G11	■	E9	■
			,		■						■		■
A10	G1	E3	,	G6	■	H13	D4	G12	G5	E14	■	D12	
			,		■						■		■
A1	F7	F9	■	D5	A13	C2	C8	■	H3	H10	H11	C7	B6
			■				■						

17. BRIDGES

Building bridges to develop the rail network in this country and abroad has been vital through the centuries.

In each case, find a word that bridges the two words provided. The answer must link to the end of the first word and go in front of the second word.

1 FUR (_ _ _ _) DISTANCE

2 CORN (_ _ _ _ _) DAY

3 DOWN (_ _ _ _) SIDE

4 HEAD (_ _ _ _) SLIDE

5 MAIN (_ _ _ _ _ _) LINED

18. POINTS

Find a single four-letter railway-linked word that can go in front of all the letter groups on the tracks and create new words.

Clue: A warning signal?

O N

R A N T

S H I P

19. SPLITS

One of the greatest challenges to the pioneers of the railways was the landscape itself, and the words in this puzzle reflect that.

In each of the lines of letters below there are two words of equal length with a railway link. The letters are in the correct order chronologically. What are the words?

1 B S U I T O L D N E

2 P E S A T E K E P S

3 C R I A V N A L E R

4 H I V L I L S E W S

5 S P S H A O D E V E L S

20. THREE WAY

There are THREE WAYS to get to your destination with three clues. You are heading for the terminus of a famous early railway.

1 A gent

  2 A treasure box

    3 A Royal cipher

21. HARD GRAFT

The building of the Settle to Carlisle line involved a tremendous amount of physical hard graft. Here's your chance to put a shift in and try to reconstruct the empty grid. Put all the listed words back in place to read either across or down. There is one word that is left over when the frame is completed. What is it?

3 Letters

AXE   BAR   CUT   DIG   PIN

4 Letters

AXLE   DENT   HELP
LOAD   ROCK   ROPE
RUNS   TURN   WORK

5 Letters

BRAWN   CHAIN   HILLS
ROUTE   SKIES   SPADE
STEAM   STONE

6 Letters

BOILER   CREATE
GREASE   GROUND
HIRING   RIVERS
SETTLE   SHOVEL
SPEEDS   SUMMIT
TUNNEL   WEIGHT

7 Letters

APPLEBY   BRIDGES
NAVVIES   TRAFFIC
VIADUCT

8 Letters

CARLISLE   FLOODING
GARSDALE

9 Letters

DANGEROUS

10 Letters

LANGWATHBY
RIBBLEHEAD

11 Letters

ARMATHWAITE

12 Letters

CONSTRUCTION

13 Letters

KIRKBY STEPHEN

22. STATIONGRAM

Rearrange the letters to spell out the name of a station.

23. THE RAILWAY CHILDREN

Family excursions became much more popular towards the end of the nineteenth century. Railways enabled many more people to take holidays and excursions, including women and families.

On this particular day, a family consisting of a grandmother, two mothers, two daughters and a granddaughter boarded the train bound for the seaside. They all needed a seat each. What is the minimum number of seats that needed to be booked?

24. WHEEL-RIGHT

Solve the railway-linked clues, and write the answers clockwise back in the WHEEL. The clues are not in the RIGHT order, and may overlap by one or more letters with the word in front or behind them. It's up to you to work out which is the RIGHT way to fill the WHEEL. The first letter of Answer 1 is in place, and we give you the length of each answer to help you along the way.

Country where the Shimla railway was built (5)

Sketch or drawn plan (7)

Device to keep you warm on a train (6)

Came together at an agreed location (3)

Scottish river with a famous bridge (5)

Tract of undeveloped land (7)

Express train which doesn't stop on its journey (7)

Layer of grass with earth (4)

With an uneven surface (5)

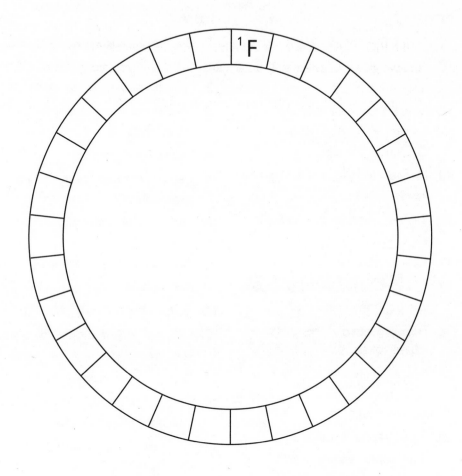

25. CRYPTIC

Get on board to answer these cryptic clues!

ACROSS

3 Stick for rail workers? (5)

7 Sounds like a composer at the door (6)

8 Fruit transported from the Garden of England or the Garden of Eden? (6)

10 Men let raid happen causing accident (10)

11 Parts of carriages on the move (4)

12 Railway trail (5)

13 Space trot exercise for the speed competition observer (9)

16 Freshly created – provided food (7)

21 Reading matter for the journey; could they be stores of explosive material? (9)

22 Payments for outdoor entertainments, we hear? (5)

23 Plain countryside (4)

24 The start of Mrs Christie's 4.50 train journey, with a bear on board? (10)

26 Teaches locomotives (6)

27 Becoming tenser, goes into tunnel (6)

28 Teams produce energy (5)

DOWN

1 Swerves through any professions (7)

2 Lend ticket before you travel (7)

3 Sounds like a confined space to vend tickets (4)

4 Secure high speed (4)

5 Place is prepared for something exceptional (7)

6 Log more adjustment for knee comfort (3,4)

9 New pelmets made for Bristol station (6,5)

14 Team heard at railway hub (4)

15 Cab, but outside the station not in it! (4)

17 Duck famous record-breaker (7)

18 Party I'd celebrated for twenty-four-hour excursion (3,4)

19 Great Ma revisited seaside destination (7)

20 Toured south initially but there were changes to the itinerary (7)

24 Overtake mountain route (4)

25 Change time for something on the menu (4)

26. THE ACCUMULATOR

Special agent, code name **Rocket**, has to find a left luggage locker at London's **King's Cross** station, which contains a secret message. He has been told that clues to the four-figure number of the locker will be revealed in a series of seemingly innocent station announcements. By the time you have finished the book you will have decoded the four clues and will have located the locker number. The answer appears at the end of Section Four solutions.

Here is the first of these:

Which clue will **Rocket** pick up from this announcement?

'This train will be delayed by a quarter of an hour. Some of our drivers have been taken ill.'

Woof!

There is a long history of man's best friend taking journeys by train. From the earliest days of the passenger railways, travellers expected to bring their dogs with them, but nineteenth-century travelling conditions for the dogs were poor. Their crates could be buried under luggage, there was no guarantee of fresh water or food on long journeys and the noise and shaking were traumatising. When Charles Cruft started running dog shows in the 1880s, he was frustrated by the conditions dogs would arrive in at the shows after travelling by train, so he approached the LNWR to build a special carriage just for dogs. The dog carriage had twenty-six kennels with zinc floors for easy cleaning, plus an attendant and a water supply. It cannot have been a peaceful journey for the attendant!

Section Two

EXTRAORDINARY FIRSTS

EXTRAORDINARY FIRSTS

Every railway journey has a beginning. Not just a place, but also a first. Railway inaugurations were usually magnificent events, and the opening of the Stockton and Darlington Railway was no exception. On 27 September 1825 George Stephenson's *Locomotion* hauled the inaugural train consisting of a passenger coach and some thirty wagons into which more than 500 passengers crammed. Two of the wagons were dedicated to a musical band and crowds in their thousands came to see the train along its journey.

Not every inauguration went to plan though. The opening of the Liverpool and Manchester Railway in 1830 was an especially tragic case, being marred by the death of MP William Huskisson. He was climbing up the steps of the Prime Minister Duke of Wellington's carriage to escape from the path of an oncoming train hauled by *Rocket*, when the unlatched door swung open, leaving Huskisson dangling in the path of the locomotive. Unsurprisingly, the accident brought the events of the day to an early close with the passengers heading home in a sombre mood.

Most inaugurations, however, went ahead without major incidents and although railway building was mostly finished by the end of the nineteenth century, the inaugurations were not. Into the twentieth century, the railway companies had become savvy to the advertising potential of an inaugural run to launch a new service or train. From 1923, the Big Four railway companies – the Southern, the Great Western (GWR), the London and North Eastern (LNER) and the London, Midland and Scottish (LMS) – were household names. Their most famous trains, like *The Flying Scotsman* and *Golden Arrow*, even more so. The following are the inaugural journeys behind some of the famous names in railway travel.

Thomas Cook

The once giant name in the world of package holidays is more frequently associated with aviation than railways. However, Thomas Cook began its life with a railway journey organised by its namesake in 1841. Thomas Cook, aged thirty-two, was a committed member of the temperance movement. The growing campaign sought to persuade people, especially from working-class backgrounds, to cease drinking alcohol. Much of the movement revolved around substituting drinking with alternative forms of entertainment: supporting libraries, museums, parks, gardening, brass bands and cocoa houses. Thomas Cook thought the railways could be mobilised as another tool in the arsenal of the temperance movement.

On 5 July 1841, Cook organised an excursion from Leicester to the nearby town of Loughborough. Onto the train of mostly open wagons, around 500 members of the temperance movement crammed together for the journey. They paid just one shilling each for the return journey. In Loughborough, the group wearing ribbons and rosettes were joined by local members of the temperance movement and others who had travelled from further away. They marched around the town, played music and games, and danced, followed by plenty of speeches, before they eventually returned home. Although not even Cook knew it at the time, it was the first journey of what would eventually become a powerhouse of the tourism industry.

Over the next decade he began organising ever more elaborate excursions across the country and supporting the establishment of temperance hotels, which offered a safer night's sleep compared to most urban inns, while remaining affordable. In 1851, Cook made great success from organising excursions to the Great Exhibition at the Crystal Palace. With the support of his son, John, the business grew ever larger, organising tours across Britain and Europe. John did not share his father's zeal for the temperance movement, having much more of a head for business himself, and so under his co-leadership, the business grew into one of the largest travel companies in the world until it collapsed in 2019. The business may have died but the name and brand lives on, all owing its genesis to one journey in 1841.

The world-famous *Flying Scotsman*

The LNER's *Flying Scotsman* is the world's most famous locomotive, but why? It was the first locomotive to achieve an authenticated steam speed record of 100mph, but that alone does not explain its fame. The overall rail speed record for a train was 130mph, and that was set three decades earlier. Plenty of other steam locomotives surpassed the *Flying Scotsman* record and today's reigning speed record holder, LNER's A4 *Mallard*, is famous, but it still does not equal *Scotsman*'s recognition. However, a tremendous part of the aura that surrounds the name *Flying Scotsman* comes not just from the locomotive, but from the similarly titled train, *The Flying Scotsman*.

It is probably worth stopping here to explain the difference between a locomotive and a train, and why the word 'the' has so much significance. Most simply, a locomotive is the vehicle that contains the engine that powers a train. All the connected vehicles (the locomotive plus the carriages and wagons) are what is collectively referred to as the train. When locomotives are given names, they are to some extent personified. Conventions of language evolve and change over time, but in the same way that it would seem strange to prefix 'the' to a person's name, railway enthusiasts are endlessly irritated when 'the' is prefixed to the name of a locomotive. For our purposes, though, the convention will help to distinguish between the locomotive *Flying Scotsman* and the train *The Flying Scotsman*.

The train's fame was born out of rivalry. Between London and Scotland there were two major competing routes on the east coast and the west coast. The companies that ran those two routes viciously competed over passengers, touting the speed and comfort of their trains. The train that would become *The Flying Scotsman* began its life in 1862 with the launch of the *Special Scotch Express*. The train used the east coast route with simultaneous departures from London King's Cross and Edinburgh at 10.00 a.m. *The Flying Scotsman* quickly became the unofficial name for the service, and it was later adopted as its official name.

When the LNER took over the service at the company's formation in 1923, the train was already cemented as its fastest and most prestigious. Passengers aboard the train could always expect the LNER's best locomotives and most luxurious carriages. Passengers could experience sumptuous meals in the restaurant cars, watch films in the cinema coach, listen to the radio by hiring a set of headphones, grab a haircut in the salon or even hire a secretary to type their work via a Dictaphone. In 1924, the LNER sent one of its new express passenger locomotives to the British Empire Exhibition and, in a brilliant publicity move, named it after its most famous train, instantly promoting that engine to become the LNER's most famous.

On 1 May 1928, *The Flying Scotsman* entered its golden era with the launch of a non-stop service. The departures of the inaugural trains, both leaving the capitals at the usual 10.00 a.m., were witnessed by huge crowds. *Flying Scotsman* hauled the northbound train and was seen off by the Lord Mayor of London, with many journalists and dignitaries aboard. The new non-stop service was made possible by an innovation by engineer Sir Nigel Gresley, who added a corridor to the tender to allow the locomotive's crew to swap midway through the journey. A single crew simply could not be expected to handle the demands of shovelling an average of a ton of coal per hour over the full eight-hour journey. The train set a record for the longest scheduled non-stop train in the world, yet another record that contributed to the train's fame. *The Flying Scotsman*, although no longer non-stop, still runs between London and Edinburgh – the longest running titled train in the world.

The upturned bathtub's near-miss

The rivalry over the Anglo-Scottish expresses was one of the greatest in railway history. The competition between the LNER and the LMS was the source of many dramatic events on Britain's railways in the 1930s. In 1937, both companies launched new streamlined trains to link London and Scotland. The LNER's service was named *The Coronation* and the LMS's

The Coronation Scot (King George VI's coronation was shortly before the trains launched). At the time, the LNER held the British speed record for a steam locomotive of 113mph set the previous year. What better way to launch the new train than by breaking the record using one of the new locomotives specifically designed for the new service?

On 29 June, members of the press were invited aboard a special train to preview the LMS's new service which would launch the following week. The brand-new locomotive 6220 *Coronation*, in a fetching blue and silver livery, headed the train of dedicated matching carriages. The locomotive was streamlined to compete with the A4s of the LNER, although detractors derided the styling as an upturned bathtub. As the train headed towards Crewe, the speed climbed upwards. Two miles from the station, 114mph was recorded, breaking the LNER's record.

However, to achieve the phenomenal speed, the driver Mr Clarke was pushing his train to the limit. Not just the limit of how fast it could go, but also how quickly it could stop. At the entrance to Crewe station lay a set of points for which the speed limit was just 25mph. Braking sharply, the train crossed the points at a whopping 57mph. It was a miracle that the train was not thrown off the rails. Certainly, many other accidents have involved much less excessive speeds on similar track. In the event, the worst outcome was some shaken journalists and broken crockery. It was only luck that averted disaster.

1. COGNITIVE

The cogs in the wheel all have SIX letters. Solve the railway-linked clues below. Some answers are written clockwise and some anti-clockwise – it's up to you to work out which is the correct way. The first letter of Answer 1 is in place.

1 The elder of the famous Stephenson family

2 Locomotive that took part in the opening of the Liverpool–Manchester Railway

3 Materials such as iron and steel

4 Warns of danger

5 Added coal to the furnace

6 Promise, especially to refrain from consuming alcohol

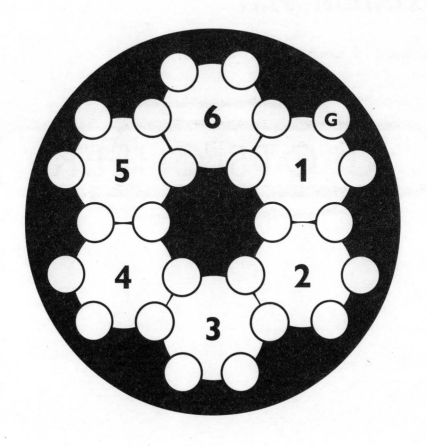

2. STATIONGRAM

Rearrange the letters to spell out the name of a station.

CLOTS CHEER

3. SECTION SUM

Can you work out the total of the sum below? All the facts are contained in the text at the start of this section.

The date in July that **Thomas Cook** organised his first excursion PLUS the date in May 1928 that *The Flying Scotsman* launched its non-stop service PLUS the number on the hour when *The Flying Scotsman* left Edinburgh and King's Cross simultaneously in 1862?

4. A TO Z

This puzzle looks like an ordinary crossword. However, there are no clues. The letters A to Z are each represented by a number instead. We have given you the numbers that represent the letters in the word **FIRST** to start you off. All the answers in the crossword grid have a railway link. Most answers are made up of a single word, but also look out for two words that are often coupled together!

The checklist below will help you to keep track of the letters you have found.

1 = **F**, 2 = **I**, 3 = **R**, 4 = **S**, 5 = **T**,

6 = , 7 = , 8 = , 9 = , 10 = , 11 = , 12 = , 13 = , 14 = , 15 = , 16 = , 17 = , 18 = , 19 = , 20 = , 21 = , 22 = , 23 = , 24, = , 25 = , 26 = .

	26		12		4			13		19		3		
3	13	4	20	3	5		1	2	17	5	23	3	13	4
	24		7		10			2		1		12		
15	20	18	13		1	2	3	4	5		1	24	10	8
	11		3		1		13			13		2		
5	2	16	13	4		2	5	2	18	13	3	10	3	25
	5		21		9		23		13		4			
	25			21	20	20	3	7	10	25			13	
			4		23		18		3		12		22	
1	10	4	5	5	3	10	2	18		8	3	20	23	12
	3		13				18		13		20		2	
11	3	13	7		19	13	8	2	18		16	10	12	4
	2		10		20			6		20		12		
20	26	13	3	24	20	10	21		20	23	5	4	13	5
	13		21		14			25		13		21		

5. CHANGING STATIONS

Each wheel contains six individual letters. Two letters are shared with the other wheels. One question mark sign, which indicates a letter common to all three words, appears in the centre. Decide on the mystery letter, then use the letters to make three railway stations with **NINE** letters in each.

Set the wheels in motion and begin the journey, which will take you to the beauty of the Scottish landscape.

1 _ _ _ _ _ _ _ _

2 _ _ _ _ _ _ _ _

3 _ _ _ _ _ _ _ _

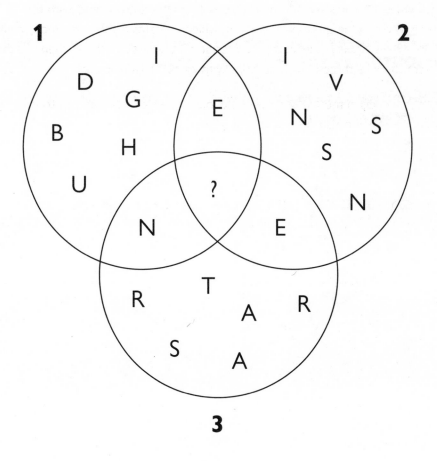

6. ROUTE FINDER

The five main stations on this railway network are marked A, B, C, D and E.

You can journey on any piece of track, but every station that you call at must be **SOUTH** of the station that you have just come from.

Given that you do not have to visit every station, how many different ways are there of getting from station A to E?

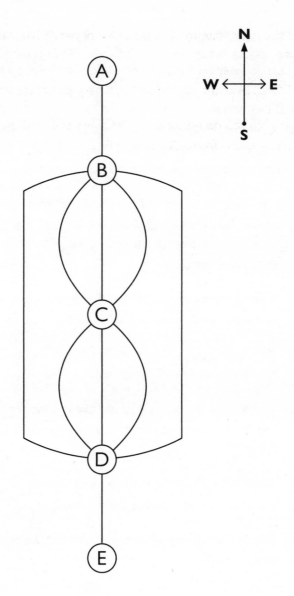

7. AWAY DAYS

The development of the railway network meant that families could actually travel to places outside their own locality. They could plan trips and enjoy away days making visits to places of interest.

Each of the five families are enjoying a journey out on the train. Each group travels a different distance by rail. They all have different areas of interest when they make their visits. Being British, the weather is a vital factor in any day out. Each family came across a different type of weather.

Use the information below to fill in the upper grid. When you find a piece of positive information put a tick in the correct box. Put a cross when you have found a piece of negative information. Cross-refer until you can complete the box at the foot of the page.

1 It was perhaps fortunate that the Brown family were visiting the shops and were under cover as the weather became very thundery.

2 The family going to visit friends had the shortest rail journey. They were not the family caught in the rain.

3 The Arnold family travelled half the distance of the family who visited the gardens and enjoyed some sunny weather. This was not the Close family.

4 The family visiting the theatre had a journey of 30 miles. They weren't the ones to have cloudy weather.

5 The Dawson family were not heading to the theatre, but they did find it misty.

		Weather					Distance					Visiting				
		Cloudy	Misty	Rainy	Sunny	Thundery	10 miles	24 miles	30 miles	48 miles	56 miles	Friends	Gardens	Museums	Shops	Theatre
Family	Arnold															
	Brown															
	Close															
	Dawson															
	Ewing															
Visiting	Friends															
	Gardens															
	Museums															
	Shops															
	Theatre															
Distance	10 miles															
	24 miles															
	30 miles															
	48 miles															
	56 miles															

Family	Weather	Distance	Visiting

8. RAILWAY READS

One attraction of a railway journey was that it gave travellers an opportunity to read. Indeed, many absorbing works of fiction were about trains themselves.

Work out the titles of these great railway reads. The vowels in the titles have been removed and the letters regrouped, although they are in the correct sequence. The novels all feature the excitement of rail travel between their pages.

1 MRD   RNT   HRN   TXP   RSS.

2 STR   NGR   SNT   RN.

3 THG   RLN   THT   RN.

4 THT   HRT   YNN   STPS.

5 THM   YST   RYF   THB   LTRN.

9. LINE NINE

Each number from 1 to 9 represents a different letter of the alphabet. Solve the clues and write the letters in the appropriate spaces in the grid. When all nine letters are in place you will find a well-known picturesque destination on the Highland main line.

1	2	3	4	5	6	7	8	9

Clues

A A very large town   6239

B Tar   12367

C A truck or wagon   45889

10. SEASIDE SPECIALS

The advent of the railways meant that people could go on holiday, and head for the seaside. Extraordinary firsts indeed! The names of seaside destinations with stations can all be found in the letter grid. They are all in straight lines and can go across, backwards, up, down or diagonally.

AYR	LOWESTOFT
BLACKPOOL	MARGATE
BOGNOR REGIS	NEWQUAY
BORTH	OBAN
BOURNEMOUTH	POOLE
BRIDLINGTON	RHYL
BRIGHTON	RYDE
BRIXHAM	SCARBOROUGH
BUDE	SOUTHEND
CLACTON	SOUTHPORT
CLEETHORPES	TENBY
DEAL	TORBAY
EASTBOURNE	TORQUAY
FELIXSTOWE	WEYMOUTH
HEMSBY	WHITBY
HEYSHAM	YARMOUTH
HOVE	
LOOE	

```
E  O  O  L  H  G  U  O  R  O  B  R  A  C  S
E  A  S  T  B  O  U  R  N  E  M  O  U  T  H
W  X  S  O  U  T  H  E  N  D  S  N  H  N  F
B  H  E  D  U  B  W  B  Y  Z  O  I  O  E  J
N  H  I  Z  C  Q  U  B  R  T  S  T  L  T  N
O  P  H  T  U  L  N  D  C  I  H  I  Z  A  G
T  T  E  A  B  E  E  A  G  G  X  R  D  G  T
G  F  Y  N  T  Y  L  E  I  S  H  H  E  R  R
N  O  S  A  T  C  R  R  T  Y  T  L  A  A  O
I  T  H  B  U  R  B  O  L  H  U  B  L  M  P
L  S  A  O  O  Q  W  E  Y  M  O  U  T  H  H
D  E  M  N  E  E  R  Z  O  R  M  R  P  O  T
I  W  G  Y  A  B  R  O  T  Y  R  B  P  V  U
R  O  Y  B  S  M  E  H  T  D  A  Y  R  E  O
B  L  A  C  K  P  O  O  L  E  Y  Z  O  R  S
```

11. CLOSURE

In the nineteenth century the expansion of miles of track and the opening of stations moved at a great pace. This was balanced by an extraordinary change in the twentieth century when the first major closures of lines took place. Dr Richard Beeching was chairman of British Rail in the 1960s. Known as The Beeching Axe, 2000 stations and 5000 miles of track were closed down.

Not quite so savage is our closure scheme. There are thirty-six stations all interlinked by a criss-crossing of track. SIX stations need to be closed. It must be done in such a way that every line going across, every line going down and every diagonal line never loses more than ONE station.

The first TWO stations for the axe are marked.

Which of the others will be for the chop?

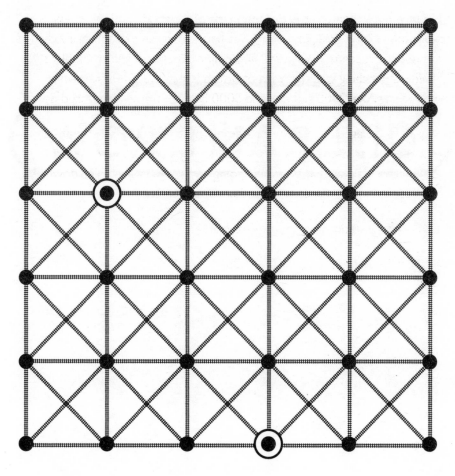

⊙ Stations to close

12. STATIONGRAM

Rearrange the letters to spell out the name of a station.

GIN RANT ROW

The Capture of Winston Churchill

Winston Churchill began his career in his twenties with a curious mix of military adventure, journalism and politics. With war looming in South Africa, Churchill travelled to Cape Town in October 1899 as a journalist for the *Morning Post*. Within weeks he joined an armoured train (a military train kitted out with guns and metal plates to protect its occupants) on what would prove a very eventful journey. The train was derailed and attacked by Boers. While some of the soldiers escaped, Churchill was captured and taken to Pretoria as a prisoner of war. A few weeks later, he escaped by scaling the prison wall at night and began a 300-mile journey to escape enemy territory while he was the subject of a manhunt. When he eventually made it out, concealed in a freight train, to a neighbouring neutral country, he returned to South Africa in the military and liberated the men he had left behind in the prison.

13. MAP THE JOURNEY

The eight marked railway destinations have had the letters in their names arranged in alphabetical order. Unravel the names and match them to the numbers on the map to identify four famous railway journeys. We give you a list of four journey distances. Can you match them to the journeys? Happy travelling!

ACEILLRS

ADGLOSU

AGHINSST

CHIIPSW

CHINORW

DLNNOO

EELSTT

EINOPRRT (two words)

Distances	Journeys
15.5 miles	1 to 2
40 miles	3 to 4
55 miles	5 to 6
72 miles	7 to 8

14. WHERE AM I?

Use the riddles to work out the letters that name the station at the end of the journey.

My first is in **SPACE**
But isn't in **SEAT**.

My second is in **RACE**
But isn't in **HEAT**.

My third is in **SPEED**
And also in **BRAKE**.

My fourth is in **WATER**
But isn't in **LAKE**.

My fifth is in **CURVE**
And also in **BEND**.

My journey is over,
It's come to an end!

15. AVERAGE

On your journey outward you travel at an average speed of 90 miles per hour. A few days later, when you come to make the return journey some track maintenance is being carried out. The average speed on the return journey is down to 30 miles per hour.

What was the average speed for the entire journey?

16. QUOTABILITY

Solve the clues and put your answers in the correct squares in the grid. All the answers have EIGHT letters. When the upper grid is complete the first column reading down will reveal the first name of a character in *The Importance of Being Earnest* by Oscar Wilde. Transfer the keycoded letters to the lower grid and complete a quotation by her, which begins, 'I never travel without my diary. One should always have..........'

1 A stretch of railway that slopes from the horizontal

2 These make a shrill sound when blown and were used as signals

3 Asks a question to find information

4 Humorous alternative title – e.g. the Canterbury/Whitstable line was known as the Crab and Winkle line

5 Space or measure between two locations

6 Railway owner, who organised the running of the line

7 Citrus non-alcoholic drink, as may have been preferred by pioneer Thomas Cook's temperance movement

8 The way into a station

9 The City and South London Railway is now known as this line on the London Underground

Grid (columns A–H, rows 1–9) — empty.

D2	G6	C7	H5	D5	E9	E3	E4	A1	■	
H2	G3	F5	H3	F4	F6	E1	D7	F8	E6	F2	■
D9	A6	■		G9	H4	E5	G7	■	B9	B8	■
H1	B2	H7	■	C8	F3	E8	B4	H9	■	

17. BRIDGES

Building bridges to develop the rail network in this country and abroad has been vital through the centuries.

In each case, find a word that bridges the two words provided. The answer must link to the end of the first word and go in front of the second word. There is one proper name created.

1 DARLING (_ _ _) SURE

2 UNDER (_ _ _ _) PLATE

3 BRASS (_ _ _ _) STAND

4 DART (_ _ _ _ _) GAME

5 LIFE (_ _ _ _) TABLE

18. POINTS

Find a single four-letter railway-linked word that can go in front of all the letter groups on the tracks and create new words.

Clue: One of many new to the skyline in the railway era?

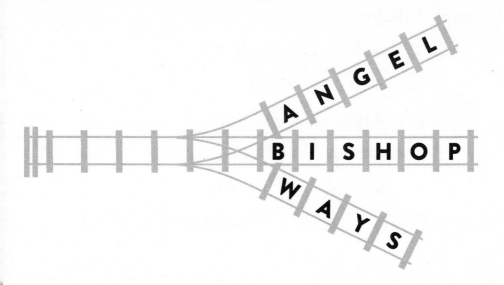

19. SPLITS

The arrival of the railways, and the work of campaigner Thomas Cook, meant that 'ordinary' folk could travel safely away from home for the first time.

In each of the lines of letters below there are two words of equal length with a railway link. The letters are in the correct order chronologically. What are the words?

1 T O T R U I R S P S

2 Q S E U E A U T S E

3 H S L O E E T E L P

4 A I W I S N L D E O W S

5 E L A V E N U N T S C H

20. **THREE WAY**

There are THREE WAYS to get to your destination with three clues. You are heading for a resort with a musical link to pirates.

1   Take some small change

    2   Insert into this the alphabet in reverse

       3   Add a compass point

21. DINING CAR

The first dining car in England was run by GNR on 1 November 1879. These restaurants on the move became the watchword for fine dining – delicious food, beautiful table linens, expensive silver cutlery and delicate china. Relive the splendour of this Golden Age.

The listed words can all be fitted back into the letter grid. They are all in straight lines and go across or down.

3 Letters
EAT   FED   USE

4 Letters
FISH   MEAT   OPEN

5 Letters
CATER   COCOA   CREAM
SLICE   STAFF   STOUT

6 Letters
BOTTLE   BUFFET
CRUETS   DRINKS
GOBLET   MUFFIN
PEOPLE   RAGOUT
SALVER   SCONES
SEATED   SWEETS
TUREEN

7 Letters
BASKETS   CARAFES
PLATTER   TEATRAY

8 Letters
ASSISTED   CONSOMME
HOT WATER

9 Letters
BEEFSTEAK   CAKESTAND
CONDIMENT   SAUCEBOAT
SERVIETTE

10 Letters
BREAKFASTS
TABLECLOTH

11 Letters
CHEESEBOARD
DINNER PLATE
REFRESHMENT

13 Letters
VEGETABLE DISH

14 Letters
COCKTAIL SHAKER

22. STATIONGRAM

Rearrange the letters to spell out the name of a station.

PLANT BEARS

23. THE JEWEL IN THE CROWN

The rivalry between railway companies competing to be the fastest between England and Scotland is the stuff of railway legend. Events reached fever pitch in 1937 when LNER and LMS each launched new trains linking the two countries.

In this grid we want to transport you back to 1937 as you discover the number of a locomotive that became its company's crowning glory that year. Fill the grid below so that the digits 0–8 appear in each row, each column and each 3 x 3 square. When the grid is complete take the letters in the shaded squares, reading left to right top to bottom to reveal its number.

6	5				4	8	2	
	0	2	3				4	1
1	7	6						
				1		2		4
			8		6		5	
			4		2			
3	2	8		0				
						6	0	

24. WHEEL-RIGHT

Solve the railway-linked clues, and write the answers clockwise back in the WHEEL. The clues are not in the RIGHT order, and may overlap by one or more letters with the word in front or behind them. It's up to you to work out which is the RIGHT way to fill the WHEEL. The first letter of Answer 1 is in place, and we give you the length of each answer to help you along the way.

S stands for this in the initials LMS (8)

Isambard Brunel's middle name (7)

Joins together, as when rail companies combine (6)

Curved glass roof such as at Edinburgh's Waverley station (4)

Tool like a spade for shifting coal (6)

Rate of movement (8)

London, Glasgow, Bristol, for example (4)

Important railway junction, now home of the National Railway Museum (4)

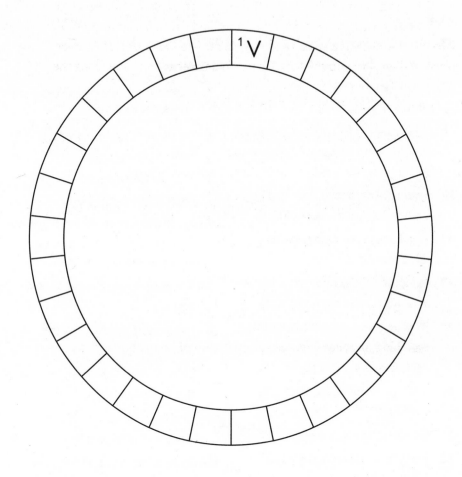

25. CRYPTIC

Get on board to answer these cryptic clues!

ACROSS

3 Routs concerning new holiday journeys (5)

7 Raver I misled to reach a destination (6)

8 Raw material in a spin at the first North West passenger terminus (6)

10 Liverpool station, a thoroughfare with a tropical flavour? (4,6)

11 Appear to take a step in this direction (4)

12 Inexpensive day return, to relieve an ache, a pain, apparently (5)

13 Rants extensively before harbour town and provides conveyance (9)

16 A break is not allowed on this train (3,4)

21 Orators' dais at the station (9)

22 Partly tax less to make wheel spindles (5)

23 Below the ankles we hear, but a noteworthy achievement (4)

24 Monarch is tetchy at north London terminus? (5,5)

26 A carpenter by another name may get back on the train later (6)

27 Patronage in the usual way (6)

28 Elephant's luggage? (5)

DOWN

1 Fighter if out of order, will be carried as cargo (7)

2 He powers up the engine, but is there in an emergency (7)

3 Trial that established speed records (4)

4 In rail pioneering terms this royal ceremony precedes one from north of the border (4)

5 Try at tempting them to set a first (7)

6 Keep company with Victoria's influential spouse? (7)

9 Look to hire fresh men to staff this buffet car (11)

14 The train arrives at this time, whichever way you look at it! (4)

15 So how did this London area appear to become a Birmingham maintenance depot? (4)

17 Peelers on the look out? No it's time for bed in this carriage (7)

18 Broadcasting company on the railway? (7)

19 Put forward a view of high-speed train (7)

20 Eat posh ingredients? Maybe have sandwiches and cakes here (3,4)

24 Hops from here, but nothing to do with standing on one leg (4)

25 Dismiss bag on mail train (4)

Railway Jargon and Slang

The workers who built and operate the railways developed lots of slang and jargon to describe the many complex parts of their jobs. Can you work out what these odd words mean?

1 Who was referred to as a 'bobby'?

a. A stationmaster. b. A signalman. c A ticket checker.

2 What was an 'edmondson'?

a. The sliding window fitted on old railway carriages.
b. A piece of equipment used in railway signalling.
c. A common type of railway ticket.

3 What did a 'tapper' do?

a. Jiggled the stones underneath the track to help them settle.
b. Secured tarpaulins on to open wagons.
c. Checked a train for broken wheels.

4 What was a 'triangle' used for?

a. To change the direction a train or locomotive was facing.
b. To measure small components in a railway works.
c. To warn trains that they needed to slow down.

5 What is a 'Harrington Hump' used for?

a. Decoupling freight wagons at marshalling yards.
b. To load horse-drawn carriages on to trains.
c. To help passengers with reduced mobility board trains.

6 What was a 'sprag'?

a. A piece of wood that stopped a wagon from rolling away.
b. The piece of card punched out of a ticket.
c. A paraffin-soaked rag used for cleaning engines.

7 Where could you find a 'codsmouth'?

a. On the front of a LNER streamlined locomotive like *Mallard*.
b. In special wagons built for carrying fish.
c. On water tank fillers for topping up steam engine tenders.

8 What was the 'Decapod'?

a. A carriage with ten compartments.
b. A steam locomotive with ten driving wheels.
c. A train that ran through the sea on ten wheeled legs.

9 What is a 'snifter'?

a. A type of valve on a steam locomotive.
b. A tool for quickly extinguishing the fire in a steam engine.
c. A type of sack used for carrying small parcels on trains.

26. THE ACCUMULATOR

Special agent, code name **Rocket**, has to find a left luggage locker at London's **King's Cross** station, which contains a secret message. He has been told that clues to the four-figure number of the locker will be revealed in a series of seemingly innocent station announcements. By the time you have finished the book you will have decoded the four clues and will have located the locker number. The answer appears at the end of Section Four solutions.

Here is the second of these clues:

Which clue will **Rocket** pick up from this announcement?

> 'When the weather starts to freeze rooms are available, with heating, for you to wait in.'

Section Three

BREAKING NEW GROUND

BREAKING NEW GROUND

Throughout railway history, engineers have achieved astonishing feats. They have pushed the boundaries through discovery and experimentation, out of necessity and sometimes just to prove a point. In the process, they created some amazing stories, three of which are explored below.

The blue streak

The 1930s had been an important decade for railway steam speed records. After *Flying Scotsman* became the world's first steam locomotive to achieve an authenticated 100mph in 1934, the British record was beaten several times in the next four years. By 1938 the British record holder was *Coronation* with 114mph achieved the previous year. However, the world record had left the British Isles in 1936, when on 11 May the Deutsche Reichsbahn's (German State Railways) streamlined class 5 locomotive 05 002 (it did not have a name) achieved 124.5mph between Berlin and Hamburg.

In the summer of 1938, Sir Nigel Gresley (Chief Mechanical Engineer of the LNER) was confident that his streamlined A4 locomotives could improve upon the record held by Germany. In June, the LNER had been working with the Westinghouse company to improve the braking systems on its trains. The increasing speed of the railway made it ever more important that trains could be brought to a stop effectively. Trials of the new system were being carried out and the last one was due to take place on 3 July.

When the staff from Westinghouse boarded the train that day, they had a surprise. They were informed that when the day's tests were complete, they would attempt to break the steam speed record. They were offered taxis back to their starting point, such was the risk involved in the attempt, but they all declined. With 4468 *Mallard* at the head of the train and the dynamometer car (a carriage full of scientific recording equipment) behind the engine, and the tests complete, the train began its return journey from Barkston on the East Coast Main Line. From Grantham, driver

Joe Duddington accelerated the train and heading down Stoke bank the dynamometer car recorded 125mph for around a quarter of a mile. Very briefly, the needle measured 126mph, but 125mph was sufficient to claim as *Mallard*'s new world record.

Mallard, however, did not escape the event unscathed. The friction between the moving parts, revolving at such high speeds, had created so much heat that the centre bearing had overheated. The locomotive limped to Peterborough, where another engine was called to drag the train back to King's Cross. In the capital, the journalists were ready and waiting at the station. The next day, the news was across all the front pages; the LNER had done it!

The speed record you have never heard about!

When discussing the speed records set on Britain's railways in the 1930s, there is always one small qualifier applied to them. All the records only applied to steam locomotives, not to railways as a whole. The reason for that took place in Germany in 1903.

The first electric locomotive appeared around the same time as the first electric cars in the 1830s, but as the batteries they used had a low power output, they were not a success. The first successful electric railway was invented by German engineer Werner von Siemens in 1879 and exhibited on a circular test track in Berlin. Instead of using batteries, the locomotive received power through an extra rail laid between the tracks. The new technology developed quickly, with the first electric tramway opening in Berlin in 1881 and the first electric railway in Britain opened in Brighton in 1883. The seaside resort of Blackpool, already closely associated with electricity since the start of the illuminations in 1879, followed soon after and adopted electric trams in 1885. It was also especially useful on urban underground railways where the smoke from steam locomotives was especially unpleasant. The City and South London Railway (now part of the

Northern Line) was the world's first deep level underground railway and the first to use electric traction.

Most of the early electric railways used direct current (DC). It was a much simpler system than using alternating current (AC) and needed smaller motors, but DC had its disadvantages, too. AC could be stepped up to higher voltages, enabling it to be transmitted over extended distances, making it much better on long-distance railways. In 1899 a group of German companies that understood the opportunities that electricity offered formed the *Studiengesellschaft für elektrische Schnellbahnen* (Research Association for High-speed Electric Railways, StES). They carried out research, not only into electric traction but into all aspects of running high-speed railways. This included looking at the track, power and air resistance, even incorporating military research on the aerodynamics of ballistic shells into their work. This was cutting-edge science; the era of streamlined trains was still decades away.

The research group were given approval to electrify a section of track to the south of Berlin between Marienfelde and Zossen, a length of around 14 miles. Two electric railcars were constructed, one using equipment from AEG and the other from Siemens & Halske, both long-time rivals but also both members of the StES. Tests began in 1901, achieving 99mph but tests were then paused to upgrade the track. After testing resumed in 1903, the AEG railcar achieved a phenomenal 130mph on 28 October, some 45mph faster than the contemporary land-speed record.

The tests were successful in proving what could be achieved by the technology, but they also showed how costly the system would be to implement on a broader scale. Hence why this new rail-speed record would stand for the next three decades. Only into the later decades of the twentieth century did the high-speed electric railways envisioned by this experiment become an economic reality.

Trans-Siberian record-breaker

Railway building in Britain was effectively finished by the end of the nineteenth century, so Britain's twentieth-century railway innovators were focused more on engines and trains than bridges and tunnels. The same was not true in Russia. As the end of the nineteenth century approached, not even half of Russia's modern railway network had been built. It turns out, building the world's largest railway took a long time.

The most remarkable part of Russia's railways is the Trans-Siberian, which runs from Moscow in the west to Vladivostok in the east. It is an astounding 5772 miles long and crosses seven time zones. It is the world's longest railway, and a journey along its full length takes at least six days. Occasional trains are extended to Pyongyang in North Korea, and at eight and a half days it is the longest scheduled rail journey in the world.

Constructing the behemoth started in 1891, took thirteen years to complete and required tens of thousands of workers to build, some of whom were convicts and soldiers. The construction faced many challenges, especially from the weather, which ranged from the deep freeze of Siberian winters to the muddy spring thaws and hot summers. The terrain varies from the Ural Mountains to the vast Siberian steppes, crossing many broad rivers in the process. Another challenge was Lake Baikal, the world's deepest lake and largest by volume. The lake forces the railway to take a long diversion to the south and this was the last section of the railway to be completed in 1904.

However, the lake also gave rise to one of the Trans-Siberian's most fascinating curiosities. So that trains did not need to wait for the Baikal diversion to be completed, a train ferry was built so that the trains could drive on to the ferry to cross the lake. Train ferries are not unusual, but to contend with the cold Russian winters, this train ferry was also an icebreaker. The SS *Baikal* was ordered in 1895 from shipbuilder Armstrong, Mitchell and Co in Newcastle. Upon its completion in Newcastle, the components of the finished ship were numbered, disassembled into 6900 parts, crated up and shipped to the shores of the lake where they were rebuilt. By 1900 the ferry was completed and set to work, cutting through ice up to 1.5 metres thick in winter. However, when the full railway opened in 1904, the ship's life as a train ferry was cut short, although it was retained as a backup for the not infrequent occasions that the railway around the lake was closed due to landslides. The SS *Baikal* was damaged during the Russian Civil War and subsequently broken up in 1926, but the smaller SS *Angara*, another icebreaking ship ordered alongside the train ferry, survives to this day as a museum.

The completion of the diversion around *Baikal* in 1904 was not the last construction on the Trans-Siberian, even if there was now an unbroken railway from Moscow to Vladivostok. A portion of the railway had been built across north-eastern China, but concerns grew about how secure this railway would be. Therefore, a diversion built entirely across Russian territory completed construction in 1916, adding an extra 800 miles to the route. Since then, further alternative routes have been constructed for parts of the line, as well as multiple spurs and branches that serve towns and cities that are further from the main railway. The route has also been electrified and upgraded over the last century and remains an important artery for passengers and east–west trade.

1. COGNITIVE

The cogs in the wheel all have SIX letters. Solve the railway-linked clues below. Some answers are written clockwise and some anti-clockwise – it's up to you to work out which is the correct way. The first letter of Answer 1 is in place.

1 Rates of progress over a distance

2 A pointer on a dial indicating how fast the train is going

3 Underground passage through a hill for a railway to go through

4 This was missing from Charles Dickens's Christmas table due to a rail accident

5 Give someone a job

6 Finds a solution to a problem, e.g. finding a way through a hill!

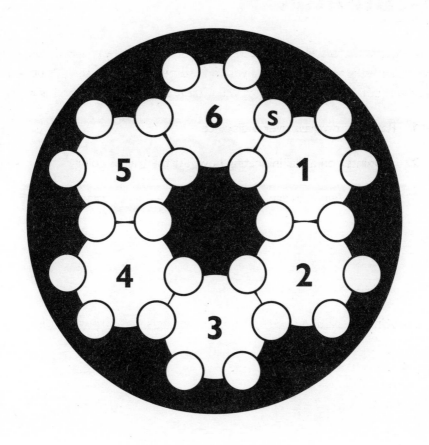

2. STATIONGRAM

Rearrange the letters to spell out the name of a station.

BEER COMMA

3. TUNNEL VISION

A train has been travelling at 60 miles per hour. Speeding through the countryside it comes to a tunnel in the mountains. The train is a quarter of a mile in length and the tunnel is 5 miles long. How long will it take for all of the train to travel through the tunnel and appear out of the other side?

4. A TO Z

This puzzle looks like an ordinary crossword. However, there are no clues. The letters A to Z are each represented by a number instead. We have given you the numbers that represent the letters in the word **VIEWS** to start you off. All the answers in the crossword grid have a railway link.

The checklist below will help you to keep track of the letters you have found.

1 = **V**, 2 = **I**, 3 = **E**, 4 = **W**, 5 = **S**,

6 = , 7 = , 8 = , 9 = , 10 = , 11 = , 12 = , 13 = , 14 = , 15 = , 16 = , 17 = , 18 = , 19 = , 20 = , 21 = , 22 = , 23 = , 24 = , 25 = , 26 = .

5. CHANGING STATIONS

Each wheel contains six individual letters. Two letters are shared with the other wheels. One question mark sign, which indicates a letter common to all three words, appears in the centre. Decide on the mystery letter, then use the letters to make three railway stations with **NINE** letters in each.

Set the wheels in motion and begin the journey, which will take you back in time to the start of one of Thomas Cook's famous journeys and onwards to two overseas destinations popular in the twentieth and twenty-first centuries.

1 _ _ _ _ _ _ _ _

2 _ _ _ _ _ _ _ _

3 _ _ _ _ _ _ _ _

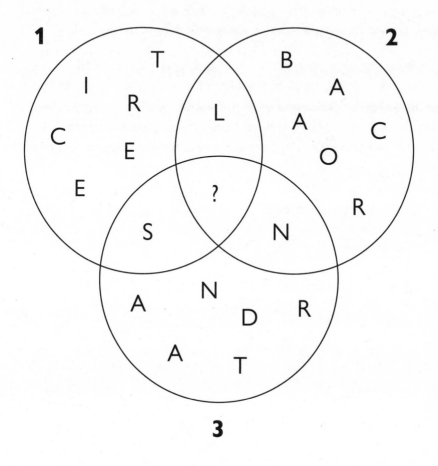

1

2

3

T
I
R
C
E
E
L
B
A
A
C
O
R
?
S
N
A
N
D
R
A
T

6. NUMBER CRUNCHING

There was tremendous drama on 3 July 1938, when *Mallard* set a new steam speed record. Time to do some number crunching in this puzzle!

Each letter has been given a numerical value from 1 to 6. The total value of each word is made up by adding the individual values. No two different alphabetical letters can have the same number.

D R A M A = **24**

M A I L = **14**

R A I L = **13**

D R I L L = **12**

What is the value of

M A L L A R D ?

Disaster at Soham

In the early hours of 2 June 1944, driver Benjamin Gimbert's journey involved working a train with over 400 tons of high-explosive bombs. As he approached Soham station, he noticed a fire had developed on the first wagon of the train. Thinking quickly, he directed his fireman James Nightall to uncouple the blazing wagon from the front of the train. Gimbert quickly pulled the wagon away from the train but made it little more than 100 metres before the 10 tons of bombs in the wagon exploded killing Nightall instantly and mortally wounding the station's signalman. The explosion dug a crater 20 metres in diameter and damaged many of the surrounding buildings, but it was a fraction of the disaster that would have happened if it were not for the actions of the enginemen. Gimbert and Nightall were both awarded the George Cross for their bravery.

7. **WIDENING HORIZONS**

Five railway enthusiasts are looking to widen their horizons. They have enjoyed many memorable trips by train in Europe, but this is the year they will be travelling further afield and embarking on a railway adventure in a completely different part of the world. From the clues, can you work out where they are heading for this journey of a lifetime, which month they are planning to go and which European railway is their current favourite?

Use the information below to fill in the upper grid. When you find a piece of positive information put a tick in the correct box. Put a cross when you have found a piece of negative information. Cross-refer until you can complete the box at the foot of the page.

1   The traveller venturing to China loves the spectacular Flam Railway, while the person going to Australia, instead of enjoying the Douro Valley this time, has booked to go away in May.

2   The West Highlands hold fond memories for the enthusiast who has booked his journey for April.

3   Mr Flag is excited about travelling on Pakistan railways. Albula is not his favourite European railway. Mr Stoker is heading for India. Neither gentleman will be going in June.

4   The experienced traveller in the Harz Mountains will go away directly before the regular visitor to Albula. He, in turn, will go away immediately before Mr Driver.

5   Mr Porter is not going to Sudan.

	Country					Month					Current Favourite				
	Australia	China	India	Pakistan	Sudan	April	May	June	September	October	Albula	Douro Valley	Flam Railway	Harz Mountains	West Highlands
Name Mr Driver															
Mr Flag															
Mr Guard															
Mr Porter															
Mr Stoker															
Current Favourite Albula															
Douro Valley															
Flam Railway															
Harz Mountains															
West Highlands															
Month April															
May															
June															
September															
October															

Name	Country	Month	Current Favourite

8. SHADED SEVEN

Building a railway that spanned seven time zones was no mean feat. In the puzzle below we give you seven quick clues at random to help you find a word related to time and endurance. We also give you the answer to the clue – but this isn't easy either as the letters have been rearranged in alphabetical order. When you have discovered the answers, place them in the grid so that the shaded squares, reading top left to bottom right, uncover the SEVEN letter name of a region that the railway crossed.

Staying power	A A I M N S T
Daybreak	E I N R S S U
Anniversary	B E E I J L U
Prospects	E F R S T U U
Wednesday	D E E I K M W
Temporary	E I I M N R T
Before	A A D E L R Y

Railway Journeys

Taking the train is always the best way to travel but can you answer these railway journey questions?

1 What is the shortest journey between two stations on the London Underground?

2 What are the *Caledonian* and *Night Riviera* the last examples of in Britain?

3 *The Flying Scotsman's* first non-stop run between London and Edinburgh was in which year?

4 What do the following all have in common: a judge's wig, a life-size cut-out of Donald Trump, a set of false teeth and an ironing board?

5 In Agatha Christie's *Murder on the Orient Express*, Hercule Poirot boards the train in which city?

6 In which country can you board the world's longest passenger train?

7 *The Night Ferry* was a luxury train between which two capital cities?

8 And in what year did it last run?

9 The longest single journey in the UK without changing trains is 785 miles long. Which two cities does it link?

9. LINE NINE

Each number from 1 to 9 represents a different letter of the alphabet. Solve the clues and write the letters in the appropriate spaces in the grid. When all nine letters are in place you will find the name of a town, which prospered during the railway boom as its trade in paper expanded.

1	2	3	4	5	6	7	8	9

Clues

A Make an intelligent guess   95631269

B Give   478269

C Exercise control   47138269

10. TRADING PLACES

Look at the trading places in the list below. There is also a list of products that came from these locations and were transported around the country, and further afield, thanks to the railways. The words in capital letters can all be found in the letter grid. They are all in straight lines and can go across, backwards, up, down or diagonally. Find them all, and then when you have done this, see if you can match each place to what it produced.

Places	Products
BURTON	BEER
CORNWALL	CAKE
CROMER	CHEESE
ECCLES	COAL
KENT	COTTON
MANCHESTER	CRAB
MELTON MOWBRAY	HOPS
NEWCASTLE	JET
NORFOLK	LACE
NOTTINGHAM	LIQUORICE
OBAN	PORK PIES
PONTEFRACT	RHUBARB
SHEFFIELD	STEEL
STILTON	TIN
WHITBY	TURKEYS
YORKSHIRE	WHISKY

M	A	N	C	H	E	S	T	E	R	B	W	J	U	P
A	E	E	O	B	U	R	T	O	N	H	Y	D	L	O
H	P	L	T	Z	O	E	L	D	I	V	L	L	L	R
G	O	T	T	B	T	A	J	S	K	E	A	I	O	K
N	N	S	O	O	C	N	K	P	I	W	Q	L	B	P
I	T	A	N	E	N	Y	O	F	N	U	Z	R	A	I
T	E	C	A	R	E	M	F	R	O	L	A	D	N	E
T	F	W	S	I	Y	E	O	R	F	B	H	T	R	S
O	R	E	T	H	H	C	I	W	U	O	I	U	O	C
N	A	N	E	S	S	C	T	H	B	N	L	R	P	R
L	C	O	E	K	E	L	R	I	A	R	T	K	E	O
A	T	K	L	R	K	E	N	T	R	L	A	E	T	M
O	A	E	Z	O	R	S	N	B	C	N	B	Y	U	E
C	H	B	J	Y	T	I	G	Y	H	O	P	S	O	R
S	T	I	L	T	O	N	L	E	E	S	E	E	H	C

11. SPEED TEST

In this puzzle, letters have been replaced by shapes. The code is constant for all the groups. Each group makes a word linked to the race for greater SPEED that fed the rivalry on the London to Scotland routes.

The first group of shapes stands for the word SPEED.

Set yourself a time trial to work out what the other groups stand for!

1 ▲ ◻ ❄ ❄ ❄

2 ▲ ▼ ❄ ❄ ◻

3 ▼ ❄ ▲ ▼ ▲

4 ▲ ▼ ❄ ❀ ○

5 ❄ ❀ ▼ ❄ ▲

6 ❄ ❀ ▲ ▼ ❄ ▲ ▼

12. **STATIONGRAM**

Rearrange the letters to spell out the name of a station.

13. MAP THE JOURNEY

The eight railway stations marked on the map have had the letters in their names arranged in alphabetical order. Unravel the names and match them to the numbers on the map to identify four famous railway journeys. We give you a list of four journey distances. Can you match them to the journeys? Happy travelling!

AACEFNNORR

ABCGHOORRSU

ACEELNSTW

ADGHMOOPRT

ADHMRU

BDDEFOR

BGHINORT

KORY

Distances	Journeys
13 miles	1 to 2
25 miles	3 to 4
36 miles	5 to 6
91 miles	7 to 8

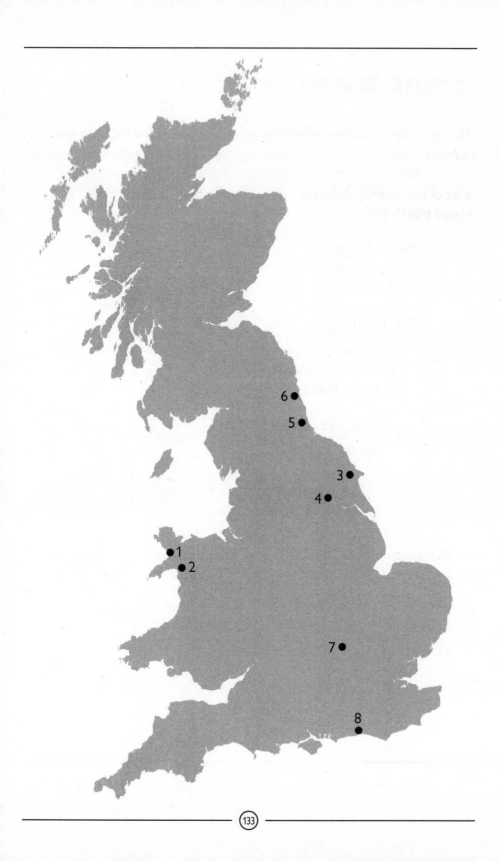

14. WHERE AM I?

Use the riddles to work out the letters that name the station at the end of the journey.

My first is in **SPRINT**
And also in **PACE**.

My second is in **LEAD**
And also in **CHASE**.

My third is in **FRAIL**
But isn't in **FAIL**.

My fourth is in **TRAIL**
But isn't in **RAIL**.

My fifth is in **HUT**
And also in **SHED**.

I am visiting Scotland.
There's no more to be said!

15. AC/DC

AC and **DC** describe types of current flow in a circuit. **AC** stands for
alternating current, and **DC** stands for **direct current**. In the words
below the letters A, C and D are missing. If you use alternating current then
the letters A and C can be added as many times as you like. If you use direct
current then the letters D and C can be added as many times as you like. Inject
an electric charge and complete the railway-related words.

1 O R R I O R

2 R G O

3 H N G E

4 O N U T O R

5 R E O R

6 O H

16. QUOTABILITY

Solve the clues and put your answers in the correct squares in the grid. All answers have **EIGHT** letters. When the upper grid is complete the first column reading down will reveal the two-word name of a train network operator. Transfer the keycoded letters to the lower grid and find a slogan from one of their advertising posters.

1 Gates at a station which stop or control entry on to the platform

2 A peak, busy period in the morning or evening (4,4)

3 Creator or pioneer, such as Brunel or Stephenson

4 The last stop on the line

5 Business or trade

6 Timetable; planned departures and arrivals

7 Very important in a development, memorable

8 Speed, swiftness

9 An unexpected event, sometimes an unfortunate one

10 Person who injects money into a project

11 A significant and notable object in a district or region

	A	B	C	D	E	F	G	H
1								
2								
3								
4								
5								
6								
7								
8								
9								
10								
11								

G6	F1	F3	■		F5	E2	B4	■		D7	H10	B8	D9	C11	■
			■					■							■

G8	B1	H11	D3	■		H9	C6	D10	■		H4	F10	H2	F11	B7	B5
				■					■							

17. BRIDGES

Building bridges to develop the rail network in this country and abroad has been vital through the centuries.

In each case, find a word that bridges the two words provided. The answer must link to the end of the first word and go in front of the second word.

1 VIEW (_ _ _ _ _) OUT

2 HIGH (_ _ _ _ _) BOAT

3 PIKE (_ _ _ _ _) SERGEANT

4 TRAM (_ _ _) WARD

5 NET (_ _ _ _) FORCE

18. **POINTS**

Find a single three-letter railway-linked word that can go in front of all the letter groups on the tracks and create new words of seven letters.

Clue: Refreshments here?

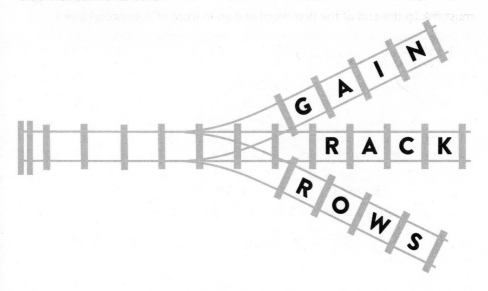

19. SPLITS

The history of railway journeys is linked with the competition between companies to provide the fastest service, and the words in this puzzle reflect this.

In each of the lines of letters below there are two words of equal length with a railway link. The letters are in the correct order chronologically. What are the words?

1 S T A S T O R P S T

2 D A H A N Z A G R E D R

3 R E S P E C O E D R D S

4 T E T R S I A T E D L S

5 S V I C U C T C O R E S Y S

20. THREE WAY

There are THREE WAYS to get to your destination with three clues. You are heading for the first stop on a holiday line and the base of the famous Great Western Railway.

1 A victory

    2 Surround this with a male child

        3 Insert 500 in Roman numerals

21. LANDSCAPE

The development of the railway network led to tracks going through many different settings.

Fit all the listed landscape-related words back in place to read either across or down.

There is one word that is left over when the frame is completed. What is it?

3 Letters

BAY   BOG   FEN   TOR

4 Letters

CRAG   EAST   ISLE
NAZE   PATH   PORT
REEF   SCAR   WEST

5 Letters

ABYSS   BROOK   CANAL
CROFT   DUNES   MOUND
NORTH   RIVER   SCENE
SHORE   SOUTH

6 Letters

COMMON   FOREST
HAMLET   MEADOW
RAVINE   STEPPE
SUMMIT   VALLEY

7 Letters

CHANNEL   CONTOUR
ESTUARY   HARBOUR
SEASIDE   STRAITS

8 Letters

DISTRICT   LANDMARK
LOWLANDS

9 Letters

LANDSLIDE

SALTMARSH

SANDBANKS

WATERFALL

10 Letters

PROMONTORY

11 Letters

COUNTRYSIDE

22. STATIONGRAM

Rearrange the letters to spell out the name of a station.

OAR GATHER

23. ICEBREAKER

The construction of the Trans-Siberian Railway, all 5772 miles of it, was not without its problems. Not least of these was the Siberian winters when icebreakers were needed to cross frozen lakes. Here the letters I C and E have been split from the rest of the word but stay in the same order. Can you cut through the ice and find the answers?

1 _ I C _ E _ _ (needed for travel)

2 _ _ I _ C _ _ E (luggage)

3 _ _ _ I C E _ _ _ _ _ (information display)

4 _ I C _ _ _ E (tool used by a navvy)

5 _ _ _ _ I C E (rail system)

24. WHEEL-RIGHT

Solve the railway-linked clues, and write the answers clockwise back in the WHEEL. The clues are not in the right order, and may overlap by one or more letters with the word in front or behind them. It's up to you to work out which is the right way to fill the WHEEL. The first letter of Answer 1 is in place, and we give you the length of each answer to help you along the way.

Nickname associated with record breaking *Mallard*,
The Blue _____ (6)

Railway tracks (5)

The mouth of a river, providing a challenge to railway builders (7)

Emperor's residence in Moscow, prior to the founding of the USSR (7)

Make progress, as with new technology in steam and electric power (7)

A junction of two railway tracks (6)

Station on the Isle of Wight opened in 1880 (4)

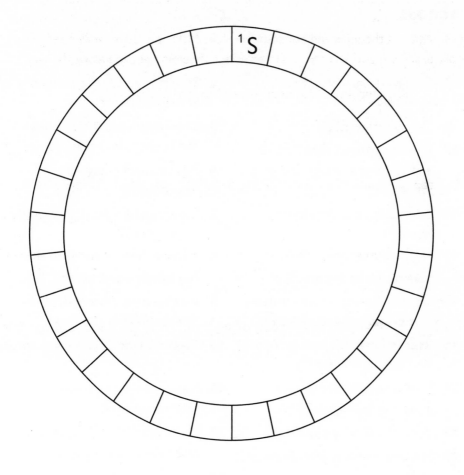

25. CRYPTIC

Get on board to answer these cryptic clues!

ACROSS

3 Asian porcelain in the buffet car (5)

7 Gentle attachment to the locomotive (6)

8 Capital terminus! (6)

10 Shamelessly spoil after Paris underground at the centre of activity (10)

11 Bale out to reach this Italian island (4)

12 Move effortlessly on where the train travels by the sea (5)

13 Set out following publicity makes a new and exciting experience (9)

16 Raise the railway above ground level turning late eve (7)

21 Point in verses goes to new ground in the Highlands (9)

22 Verify the slowing motion (5)

23 Has possession as snow is swept aside (4)

24 A favourable expectation or a possible investor (10)

26 Teach our Lydia to appear by the train every 60 minutes (6)

27 Point removed away largely north of the border (6)

28 Store the railway vehicles (5)

DOWN

1 Make more systematic and encourage expansion (7)

2 Speech at an opening ceremony where you live (7)

3 Cut farmer's produce – it will give room to lay a track (4)

4 Pals confused in European mountains (4)

5 Finances a new project – wearing just singlets (7)

6 A Great Train crime, re British Rail initially boy involved (7)

9 Viv's lad took off on the Trans-Siberian Railway (11)

14 Takes refreshment having given up a seat! (4)

15 Single network apparently in Scottish valley (4)

17 Don's won causing confusion on rack railway journey up here (7)

18 Looking forward, when it's blowing a gale I sure prefer to travel by rail (7)

19 Go after a chic debut in gangster land (7)

20 Groups of gamblers or scholars have these as their destination (7)

24 Yaps wildly but hands over the money (4)

25 Speak and lose the point, but get to the top (4)

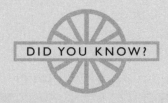

Good Railway Reads

Do you enjoy a good book (or puzzle) to while away your time on a railway journey? Before the railways, opening a book while travelling (by foot, horseback or horse-drawn carriage) was a challenge, but once the railways appeared, the much smoother ride and frequent long-distance journeys allowed the traveller plenty of opportunity to lose themselves in a good story. Of course, there was little other entertainment available. Penny dreadfuls, cheap serialised fiction aimed at the newly literate working classes, exploded as the railways grew in the 1830s. In 1848, W. H. Smith saw an opportunity and signed exclusive deals with railway companies to open bookstalls at their stations, with the first appearing at Euston station. By the end of the century there were thousands of W. H. Smith's bookstalls at stations across the country. Somehow, the Victorians missed a trick and newspaper puzzles and puzzle books did not start to appear until the 1920s and '30s, but even with modern distractions, there is still nothing better to do on a train than settling down to enjoy a good story or a challenging puzzle.

26. THE ACCUMULATOR

Special agent, code name **Rocket**, has to find a left luggage locker at London's **King's Cross** station, which contains a secret message. He has been told that clues to the four-figure number of the locker will be revealed in a series of seemingly innocent station announcements. By the time you have finished the book you will have decoded the four clues and will have located the locker number. The answer appears at the end of Section Four solutions.

Here is the third of these clues:

Which clue will **Rocket** pick up from this announcement?

> 'Luggage must not be too heavy on this train. Does your luggage weigh too much? If so, please alert the guard.'

Section Four

JOURNEYS THAT CHANGED THE WORLD

JOURNEYS THAT CHANGED THE WORLD

For most people, most of the time, travelling by train is not a momentous event. The daily commute becomes monotonous and repetitive and for those of us who travel less frequently, the destination is probably still more important than the journey. Occasionally, a trip on the train can have more personal significance. Perhaps it forms a cherished childhood memory of a day out with the family, is part of the holiday of a lifetime or a chance encounter aboard a train that blooms into a lasting relationship. However, on very rare occasions, a single journey can start ripples that change the world forever. These are three examples that did just that.

The tragic case of the royal doctor

At 5.10 p.m. on Monday, 28 January 1861, an express train departed Waterloo station bound for Portsmouth. Around 10 minutes into the journey, the train passed Epsom Junction where suddenly the train derailed. The locomotive's tender and four carriages fell down an embankment, while the fifth carriage diverged in the opposite direction and rolled onto its side. Miraculously, despite the utter destruction of the four carriages that fell down the embankment, none of their passengers were killed. The fifth carriage, however, still lay across the adjacent line. The driver knew that another express train would be approaching and so he drove his engine away from the accident to flag down the oncoming express, averting a further disaster. However, lying underneath that fifth carriage was the only fatality to have occurred that day: Dr William Baly, who had been thrown from the train and killed instantly.

Dr Baly was not well known outside of his profession, but that was not to say that he was not an important man. He was an experienced and respected physician who had gained much experience of treating infectious diseases like dysentery and cholera. In 1859 he had been appointed as extraordinary physician to Queen Victoria. Effectively, he was one of the monarch's personal doctors, part of a team that served the royal household. Even in the short period he served, he would have spent a lot of time with the Queen and

Prince Albert, and he had quickly become a trusted medical adviser. His sudden loss had a great impact on the Queen, and it was only the start of what would be a very tragic year for the royal household.

In late November of that year, Prince Albert (the Queen's cherished husband) became ill after a journey in terrible weather to inspect the military college at Sandhurst. The Queen's doctors had advised his illness was unlikely to progress to a fever and so the Prince had continued with his official duties, even though others remarked on how ill he seemed. It was not until 6 December that the possibility of typhoid was considered. The Prince died a few days later on 14 December, leaving one to wonder how events might have played out differently if Dr Baly, experienced in infectious diseases, had not died in that accident earlier that year.

It is unlikely that Baly could have done much to save the Prince. Conventional wisdom of the time was that such diseases had to be allowed to run their course and most interventions were likely to cause more harm than good. However, if Baly had recognised the symptoms earlier and advised the Prince to forgo his official duties sooner, it could have had a significant impact on events.

The year 1861 had also seen the start of the American Civil War in April. The seceded Confederate states were seeking diplomatic recognition from France and Britain and help in their war with the Union. In November the Confederacy sent two envoys aboard the British Royal Mail ship the RMS *Trent* bound for Britain and France, but it was stopped soon after departure by the USS *San Jacinto* and the envoys captured. Thus sparked a diplomatic incident that threatened to turn animosity into full-blown war between Britain and the Union. By the end of November, the British government was drafting a sternly worded letter demanding reparations for what it considered a breach of international law, a response that was likely to inflame the tensions between the two countries.

Only, that draft never made it to the USA, because before it was sent, it was passed to the Queen and then to the already ill Prince Albert who struggled to his desk to redraft the response in a far more neutral tone. There is no certainty as to how the Prince's actions changed the outcome of the Trent

Affair, but it is entirely possible that he averted a war. It's impossible to know how things would have been different if William Baly had been alive to order the Prince to rest in bed instead of re-writing that letter. How might the world have changed if Baly had not stepped into the fifth carriage of the 5.10 p.m. express to Portsmouth on that cold winter's day?

Mr Briggs's murder

On Saturday, 9 July 1864, a sixty-nine-year-old banker entered the compartment of a carriage on the North London Railway's 9.50 p.m. train from Fenchurch Street, bound for Chalk Farm. Mr Thomas Briggs had finished work early that day and, after spending the evening dining with his niece, he was now returning to his home in Hackney. Around 40 minutes later, a driver of another train returning in the other direction spotted something between the tracks. Stopping his train and sending the guard to investigate, they discovered the unconscious Mr Briggs slumped on the ballast. They dragged him down the embankment to the nearby Mitford Castle pub. Doctors were called but nothing could be done to save him. How had he come to lie on the ballast in such an injured state? Briggs's severe injuries were inconsistent with being hit by a train. The discovery later of his blood-soaked train compartment soon revealed the nature of his demise.

By the Monday morning, the newspapers were awash with all the gory details of Briggs's death, the first murder on a British train. In particular, there was the detail of a missing pocket watch and broken chain, part of which remained on Briggs's waistcoat. A reward for £200 (approximately £26,000 in today's currency) was offered for information leading to an arrest and conviction, and details of the missing watch were circulated to jewellers and pawnbrokers. A jeweller soon came forward with information about a German man who had exchanged a broken chain in his shop, and Mr Briggs's family confirmed that it was the stolen chain. However, it was not enough to identify the culprit and in the following days the press speculated wildly about the case. Meanwhile, Parliament debated yet again the safety of railway carriages. Nine days passed until another informant came forward with a name that connected to several details of the case, that of Franz Müller.

Except Müller had already left the country three days earlier, departing from London on the *Victoria*, an old wooden sailing ship bound for New York. It was the cheapest and slowest crossing available and expected to take nineteen days, but it was all that Müller could afford. However, if he made it to New York, he could surely disappear into the vast country. The only chance investigators had was to beat Müller to New York. It took two days to prepare the papers to request his extradition, giving Müller a five-day head start. However, the investigators had one advantage: the *City of Manchester* – a modern iron-hulled screw steamer. The investigators could beat Müller to New York, but only if the *Victoria* didn't find a favourable wind.

Fortune favoured the detectives and they arrived in New York ahead of Müller. The *Victoria* took a full forty days to cross the Atlantic. Müller was subsequently extradited back to Britain, found guilty of the murder (evidence suggested it was a robbery gone wrong, although this was never completely proven) and executed. However, the story did not end there, for the case had a profound impact on Victorian society.

The changes wrought by the railway revolution had included the democratising of travel for women and the working classes. That was a great thing. Anyone could travel so long as they could afford a ticket. However, Victorian society was struggling to process the shifting freedoms and power that railway travel entailed. These anxieties were beginning to coalesce around passenger safety. Railway carriages consisted of discrete compartments with their own doors. There was no corridor to link them and no method to communicate with any staff once the train left the station. Passengers were effectively trapped with each other and those other passengers could be anyone. Well, anyone that could afford a ticket, so at least a more expensive first-class compartment could be expected to keep the wealthy safe from the working classes. Right?

Except Mr Briggs was murdered in a first-class carriage and that ignited the situation into a full-blown moral panic. Despite significant reluctance on the part of the government, legislation was eventually passed four years later to mandate the inclusion of a communication cord that allowed passengers to raise the alarm. Not that it was especially effective since the cord ran outside the compartment and was accessed inconveniently via the window. Only towards the end of the century did corridor trains begin to appear, although that was more to provide access to the new restaurant cars than to improve safety. The communication cord evolved over time to something more useful and still today it is a legal requirement that carriages include a method for passengers to raise an alarm.

The journey that defined a century

The course of history was not only defined and shaped by railway travel in Britain. Events further afield also relied on train travel in a significant way. When the Russian Revolution commenced in March 1917, Vladimir Lenin (leader of the Bolsheviks) was a whole war away in neutral Switzerland. When Lenin received the message in Zurich that the Tsar had abdicated on 15 March, he and his small group of revolutionaries vowed to return to Russia and take control of the revolution. However, returning to Russia was no easy task and would require crossing Russia's enemy Germany in the midst of the First World War.

However, this was not the barrier that it would first seem. Germany was seeking all possible means to force Russia out of the war and overthrowing the new Russian government might just do that. Thus, on 9 April 1917 Lenin and his comrades set out on their journey with Germany's blessing, crossing the country in a diplomatically sealed train. Crossing the front lines was out of the question, so Lenin was bound for Sassnitz on the German Baltic coast. From there, Lenin crossed the Baltic on a ferry to neutral Sweden where he continued his lengthy journey by train to the edge of the Arctic Circle. He then crossed the frozen Torne River on sleds into Finland (then still a Russian duchy) and boarded another train for the final leg to Petrograd (the renamed St Petersburg). There he was greeted by his supporters on 16 April and six months later he and his comrades led the October Revolution that gave rise to the Soviet Union.

It was an extraordinary journey. Germany was correct that Lenin's return would precipitate Russia's exit from the war. While peace with Russia in 1918 briefly turned the war in Germany's favour, it did little to change the outcome of the war. However, the political shifts in Russia were seismic and went on to define much of the twentieth century.

1. COGNITIVE

The cogs in the wheel all have SIX letters. Solve the railway-linked clues below. Some answers are written clockwise and some anti-clockwise – it's up to you to work out which is the correct way. The first letter of Answer 1 is in place.

1 Queen Victoria's forward-thinking husband

2 Person behind the wheel of a locomotive

3 Officials on board and in charge of a train

4 Meets and welcomes

5 Guides in the right direction

6 Mr Briggs's murderer was heading for the US. What does S stand for?

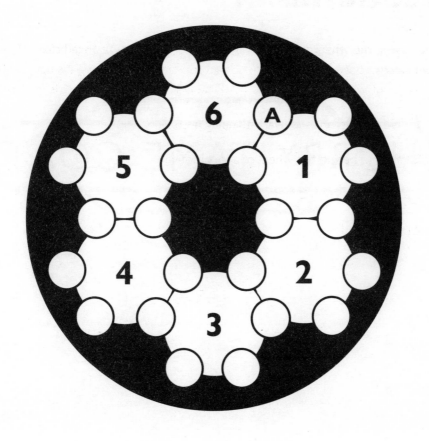

2. STATIONGRAM

Rearrange the letters to spell out the name of a station. You are looking for two words.

3. SECTION SUM

Can you work out the total of the sum below? All the facts are contained in the text at the start of this section.

The amount of reward in pounds offered for information leading to Mr Briggs's murder PLUS the number of carriages in the train that was derailed after leaving Waterloo on 28 January 1861 PLUS the date in March 1917 on which the Tsar abdicated?

4. A TO Z

This puzzle looks like an ordinary crossword. However, there are no clues. The letters A to Z are each represented by a number instead. We have given you the numbers that represent the letters in the word **WORLD** to start you off. All the answers in the crossword grid have a railway link.

The checklist below will help you to keep track of the letters you have found.

1 = **W**, 2 = **O**, 3 = **R**, 4 = **L**, 5 = **D**,

6 = , 7 = , 8 = , 9 = , 10 = , 11 = , 12 = , 13 = , 14 = , 15 = , 16 = , 17 = , 18 = , 19 = , 20 = , 21 = , 22 = , 23 = , 24 = , 25 = , 26 = .

Codeword puzzle grid (□ = black/shaded cell):

□	4	□	15	□	14	□	□	□	□	26	□	2	□	13
13	2	15	21	7	3	□	13	4	12	21	16	2	3	20
□	14	□	3	□	2	□	□	□	3	□	16	□	9	□
22	12	25	7	□	1	2	3	4	5	□	13	9	14	11
□	4	□	21	□	5	□	□	12	□	□	□	7	7	□
5	9	21	14	6	□	6	9	22	6	4	12	8	5	15
□	21	□	6	□	24	□	4	□	□	9	11	□	□	□
□	26	□	□	23	10	9	14	11	4	26	□	□	7	□
□	□	□	13	□	15	□	12	□	□	4	□	17	□	19
7	20	13	4	2	26	7	3	15	□	14	2	12	14	6
□	12	□	12	□	□	□	□	5	□	14	□	10	□	12
2	13	7	8	□	18	9	15	21	12	□	3	2	18	7
□	13	□	8	□	12	□	□	□	3	□	8	□	12	□
4	7	18	7	4	4	7	5	□	22	3	7	7	21	15
□	5	□	5	□	7	□	□	□	2	□	26	□	7	□

5. CHANGING STATIONS

Each wheel contains six individual letters. Two letters are shared with the other wheels. One question mark sign, which indicates a letter common to all three words, appears in the centre. Decide on the mystery letter, then use the letters to make three railway stations with letters in each.

Set the wheels in motion and begin the journey, which will take you to destinations in the former USSR.

1 _ _ _ _ _ _ _ _

2 _ _ _ _ _ _ _ _

3 _ _ _ _ _ _ _ _

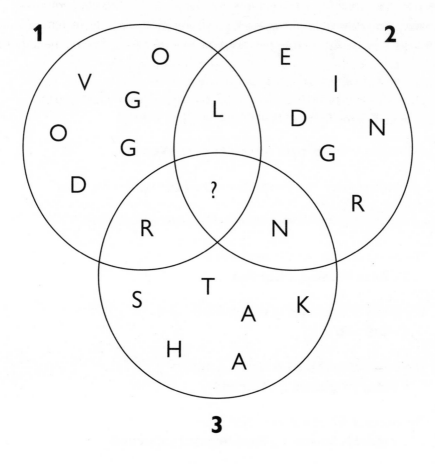

6. FROZEN TRACKS

Deep in the areas of frozen ice, there are many problems to encounter with a railway. You have to lay down the tracks entering in the bottom left grid as indicated. The railway exits in the direction indicated in the bottom right grid.

There are six types of track that can be used:

- Straight section of track running **North** to **South**.

- Straight section of track running **East** to **West**.

- Section of track that curves. There are **four** options for these.

The areas showing frozen lakes cannot be crossed by rail tracks.

The pieces of track used in section A are:
  3 x **East West**; 2 x **Curved**.

The pieces of track used in section B are:
  4 x **Curved**.

The pieces of track used in section C are:
  1 x **North South**; 2 x **Curved**.

The pieces of track used in section D are:
  1 x **North South**; 1 x **East West**; 2 x **Curved**.

The pieces of track used in section E are:
  1 x **East West**; 4 x **Curved**.

The pieces of track used in section F are:
  2 x **East West**; 2 x **Curved**.

Can you complete the plan to lay the tracks?

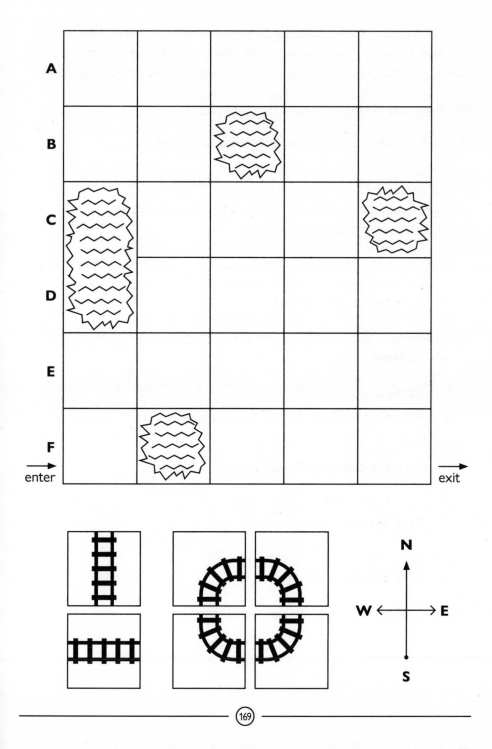

7. END OF THE LINE

The unfortunate Mr Briggs was the first victim of a murder on a British train. Fortunately, murders on trains are mostly confined to the world of novels devoured by the passengers. Five murder novel enthusiasts are travelling on a train together. From the clues, can you work out their names, the station where they leave the train, which occupation they have and which murder writer they are reading?

Use the information below so that you can fill in the upper grid. When you find a piece of positive information put a tick in the correct box. Put a cross when you have found a piece of negative information. Cross-refer until you can complete the box at the foot of the page.

1   Both Mr Ripper and the accountant stayed on the train as it went past Eskmorn. Neither of them bother with Agatha Christie novels.

2   Mr Bones, the builder, did not leave the train at Durden, the second station on the line. He was not the Ian Rankin fan who got off first at Chilsale station.

3   Miss Deeds, the tailor, was engrossed in a Dorothy L Sayers story.

4   The lawyer got out at Alesley. He was not reading a Ruth Rendell mystery.

5   Mrs Case got off the train before Mr Cheatem did.

		Station					Occupation					Author				
		Alesley	Brenton	Chilsale	Durden	Eskmorn	Accountant	Architect	Builder	Lawyer	Tailor	Christie	James	Rankin	Rendell	Sayers
Name	Mr Bones															
	Mr Case															
	Mr Cheatem															
	Miss Deeds															
	Mr Ripper															
Author	Christie															
	James															
	Rankin															
	Rendell															
	Sayers															
Occupation	Accountant															
	Architect															
	Builder															
	Lawyer															
	Tailor															

Brenton Station

Direction of travel

Name	Station	Occupation	Author

8. PLATFORM PUZZLE

A Classics student is filling time during a long holiday from university by working at his local railway station. He seizes the opportunity on his first day at work to put his Classics knowledge to the test, as he chalks the numbers of different platforms where trains would arrive and depart up on the display board. From the information below, can you work out what he wrote up for platform six? He caused total confusion of course!

Platform **EIGHT** he wrote as 1

Platform **NINE** he wrote as 1

Platform **SEVEN** he wrote as 5

Platform **FIVE** he wrote as 4

What did he write for platform **SIX**?

9. LINE NINE

Each number from 1 to 9 represents a different letter of the alphabet. Solve the clues and write the letters in the appropriate spaces in the grid. When all nine letters are in place you will find the name of a South East Asian country connected by railway.

1	2	3	4	5	6	7	8	9

Clues

A Train traveller   651193498

B Professional, skilled technician   93423998

C Planner, arranger   784532198

10. COMMUTERS

The arrival and development of the railways meant that people could travel further afield for their work, and so the daily commute was born. Find the listed words related to commuting in the list below. Some words relate to the advent of the railways (a twenty-first-century commuter might not wear a bowler hat) and some relate to the present day (you wouldn't catch a Victorian commuter with a laptop.) The words in capital letters can all be found in the letter grid. They are all in straight lines and can go across, backwards, up, down or diagonally.

ANNOUNCER
APP
BAG
BOWLER HAT
BRIEFCASE
BUFFET CAR
CAMERA
CARD
CARRIAGES
CONDUCTOR
CROSSWORD
EARPHONES
FILE
JACKET
LAPTOP
MESSAGE
NEWSPAPER
NOTEBOOK

PAPERS
PAY
PENCIL
POCKET WATCH
PURSE
SEAT
SIGN
SPECTACLES
STAND
SUIT
TABLET
TAXI
TICKET
TIMETABLE
UMBRELLA
WAIT
WALLET

P	P	A	T	H	E	R	A	C	T	E	F	F	U	B
A	O	T	I	U	S	C	X	I	W	A	I	T	B	O
P	T	C	C	Z	A	E	M	D	I	L	A	R	K	W
E	E	T	K	M	S	E	J	K	E	X	I	A	A	L
R	K	S	E	E	T	P	O	P	I	E	S	L	U	E
S	C	R	T	A	T	O	E	N	F	E	L	M	M	R
D	A	Z	B	Y	B	W	E	C	N	E	B	D	E	H
R	J	L	A	E	S	W	A	O	T	R	R	C	S	A
O	E	P	T	E	S	S	H	T	E	A	N	I	S	T
W	N	O	A	P	E	P	A	L	C	U	C	T	A	P
S	N	T	A	E	R	B	L	R	O	H	A	L	G	U
S	A	P	K	A	L	A	E	N	J	N	S	A	E	R
O	E	A	E	E	Z	G	N	Y	D	C	I	B	Y	S
R	O	L	T	J	C	A	R	R	I	A	G	E	S	E
C	O	N	D	U	C	T	O	R	P	E	N	C	I	L

11. KEY QUESTION

This station's name is made entirely from the letters found on the top row of a traditional typewriter or computer keyboard. What is it?

Clues:

- It contains FIVE letters.

- The station has been named in a previous puzzle in this book.

12. STATIONGRAM

Rearrange the letters to spell out the name of a station.

SHELTER COPE

13. MIX AND MILES

These EIGHT railway cities have had the letters in their names arranged in alphabetical order. Unravel the names and match them up to identify FOUR European railway journeys. Then finally, from the list, work out how many miles there are between the beginning and end of each journey. Happy travelling!

1 AADEMMRST

2 ACEEGHNNOP

3 ADDIMR

4 AEINNV

5 AIPRS

6 BELRSSSU

7 BILNOS

8 EHIIKLNS

Distances

642 miles

108 miles

547 miles

312 miles

Journeys

Station 1 to Station 6

Station 2 to Station 8

Station 3 to Station 7

Station 4 to Station 5

14. WHERE AM I?

Use the riddles to work out the letters that name the station at the end of the journey

My first is in **FAR**
And also in **NEAR**.

My second is in **GAUGE**
But isn't in **GEAR**.

My third is in **DESIGN**
But isn't in **INSIDE**.

My fourth is in **BRIDGE**
But isn't in **RIDE**.

My fifth is in **BUY**
And also in **PAY**.

Can you name the station
I've called at today?

15. ANNOUNCEMENTS

The station announcements below have had their vowels removed. What do the passengers need to know?

1 M N D T H G P (3 words)

2 T H R R L V S N T H L N (6 words)

3 S T N D C L R F T H D G (5 words)

4 T H S S R V C S D L Y D (4 words)

5 W P L G S F R T H N C N V N N C (5 words)

Dickens's Last Christmas Turkey

No individual had more influence on modern Christmas traditions than Charles Dickens and his book *A Christmas Carol*. However, Dickens's last Christmas was an eventful one – as far as his turkey was concerned at least. In December 1869, Dickens's reading tour manager George Dolby sent Charles a 13-kilogram turkey in a hamper conveyed by the Great Western Railway. However, the van carrying the turkey caught fire somewhere around Reading and it never made it to Dickens, who by Christmas Eve was still waiting for it. He may have been angry that he never received his turkey, but a letter in the museum's archives from Dickens reveals he bore nothing but 'unbroken good humour' towards the company for the accident. We do not know if he found another turkey for what proved to be his last Christmas dinner; he passed away six months later. And what became of that giant turkey? It was carved up and fed to the poor of Reading at 6d a portion.

16. QUOTABILITY

Solve the clues and put your answers in the correct squares in the grid. All answers have **EIGHT** letters. When the upper grid is complete the first column reading down will reveal the surname of a pioneer of the railways. Transfer the keycoded letters to the lower grid and find a quotation by him about his most famous invention.

1   Places where trains stop

2   A valve which controls the flow of steam to the engine

3   Describes a source of power for trains which is not steam or diesel

4   Raised structure at the side of the track where the train pulls in

5   Lines of bushes of hawthorn or bramble forming a barrier

6   All the people

7   Relating to the whole country; not regional

8   Beginning, setting out

9   Person who holds an authorised position in a company

10   Decade of the nineteenth century when the Forth Bridge was completed

	A	B	C	D	E	F	G	H
1								
2								
3								
4								
5								
6								
7								
8								
9								
10								

F1	G6	H2	■	H7	F4	E9	G5	H4	F6	E3	F8	B6	G10	■
			■											■
F9	H10	■	H5	D2	F3	C7	B2	■	C9	F10	E4	E8	E6	■
		■						■						■
A5	E7	D8	H1	C3	A1

17. BRIDGES

Building bridges to develop the rail network in this country and abroad has been vital through the centuries.

In each case, find a word that bridges the two words provided. The answer must link to the end of the first word and go in front of the second word. There is one proper name created.

1 HARD (_ _ _ _) MATE

    2 PORTS (_ _ _ _ _) PIECE

        3 POCKET (_ _ _ _ _) WORD

            4 WORKING (_ _ _ _ _) DISTINCTION

                5 FIRE (_ _ _ _ _) CLOCK

18. POINTS

Find a single four-letter railway-linked word that can go in front of all the letter groups on the tracks and create new words of eight letters.

Clue: mountain railways.

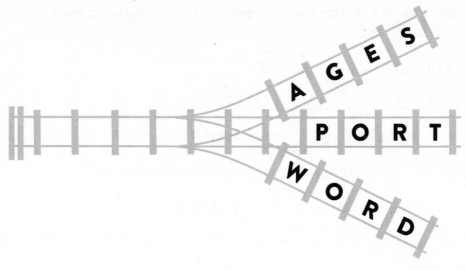

19. **SPLITS**

The expansion of rail travel to a wider audience brought with it fears for passenger wellbeing, and the words in this puzzle reflect that.

In each of the lines of letters below there are two words of equal length with a railway link. The letters are in the correct order chronologically. What are the words?

  1 D O L O I N R K

    2 P C U L O R L D

      3 A B R A L A K R M E

        4 S A S E F E C U R T E Y

          5 A G C C U E A S R S D S

20. THREE WAY

There are THREE WAYS to get to your destination with these three clues. You are heading overseas for the terminus of a narrow gauge railway, once dubbed the 'Toy Train'.

1 Three letters that sound like the seventh letter of the alphabet.

2 Insert them into a term of endearment.

3 It could be tea time.

21. PLACE TO PLACE

Look at the rail destinations below. Each destination is a terminus of a railway in an area of stunning scenery. The words in capital letters can all be fitted back into the empty grid. They are all in straight lines and go across or down.

1 ADELAIDE to PERTH

2 AJACCIO to BASTIA

3 CAPE TOWN to KIMBERLEY

4 CHICAGO to SEATTLE

5 DAMASCUS to AMMAN

6 DURANGO to SILVERTON

7 ESQUEL to INGENIERO JACOBACCI

8 GLASGOW to FORT WILLIAM

9 GUAYAQUIL to QUITO

10 JINING to TONGLIAO

11 MASSAWA to ASMARA

12 MYRDAL to FLAM

13 NULVI to PALAU

14 OSLO to BERGEN

15 PALMA to SOLLER

16 PESHAWAR to LANDI KOTAL

17 RANGOON to MANDALAY

As an extra challenge, can you match the journeys with the countries they go through?

A: Argentina/Patagonia; **B**: Australia; **C**: China; **D**: Corsica; **E**: Ecuador;
F: Eritrea; **G**: Italy; **H**: Myanmar (Burma); **I**: Norway; **J**: Norway; **K**: Pakistan;
L: Scotland; **M**: South Africa; **N**: Spain; **O**: Syria/Jordan; **P**: USA; **Q**: USA.

Railway Bridges, Tunnels and Summits

1 Which is Britain's longest railway bridge?

2 Aside from the Channel Tunnel, which is Britain's longest railway tunnel?

3 What is Britain's highest station?

4 The world's longest railway tunnel runs underneath which mountain range?

5 Which is the world's highest railway?

6 Which of the following is the odd one out: the Severn Tunnel, the Royal Border Bridge, Chepstow Railway Bridge and the Sark Viaduct?

7 What was the world's first bridge built from iron?

8 Which railway viaduct connects the names *Belgravia*, *Sebastopol*, *Jericho* and *Batty Wife Hole*?

9 And how many arches does that viaduct have?

22. STATIONGRAM

Rearrange the letters to spell out the name of a station. You are looking for three words.

MORE NEW PASTURES

23. MURDER MOST FOUL

Try to solve this Victorian murder on a train mystery.

There are six first-class compartments on the 6.00 p.m. train from Grimly Rise to Doomsday's End. Ivor Fortune – a much-hated moneylender – is the only person in first class from the start of the journey. Five more individual passengers enter first class. They get on at different stations and no one gets out until the train pulls in to Doomsday's End.

Ivor Fortune is found in his carriage. He has an empty hip flask in his hand. Gasping for breath his final words are . . . 'poisoned brandy in the flask'. He has been murdered!

The Inspector is called. Looking at the timetable and listening to the statements, he builds up a picture of where and when the passengers boarded the train and where they sat. Finally, use the Inspector's deductions to name the murderer!

—————— STATEMENTS ——————

MISS SPARROW - *'I didn't do nothing. I was only on for one stop. Been visiting my aunt and she insisted on paying for me to go first class. I nearly got in a carriage where there was already a gentleman in it. Well, I say gentleman. He told me in no uncertain terms to go away and leave him to drink his brandy in peace.'*

MAJOR ROUGH - *'I always travel in coach D.'*

LADY SMITH - *'I got into an empty carriage. I noted there was a single gentleman in each of the coaches either side of me.'*

SIR TOM O'HAWK - *'I got on at Much Havoc and saw that bounder Fortune was in coach E. I owe him some money, so I quickly moved down the platform to get as far away from him as I could. Unfortunately the very end carriage was already taken.'*

REVEREND GREY - *'Sat down to look at my Sunday sermon. Sent me to sleep at once. I must have been out for an hour, as we were leaving Stormy Down when I came to.'*

———————— • ————————

TIMETABLE

	a.m.	p.m.
Grimly Rise	....	6.00
Coldmoor	....	6.20
Wildfell Ridge	....	7.00
Much Havoc	....	7.10
Stormy Down	....	7.20
Commonrow Hill	....	7.40
Doomsday's End	....	8.00

——————— THE INSPECTOR'S DEDUCTIONS ———————

'Mr Fortune was killed by the poisoned drink in the hip flask. It was an inexpensive item, so it clearly wasn't his. Despite his vast wealth, Mr Fortune would always take something for nothing. Somebody opened the door to carriage E and offered him a gift. He took it! The poison, though fast-acting, would have taken an hour to end his life. I know who the murderer is.'

———————— • ————————

24. WHEEL-RIGHT

Solve the railway-linked clues, and write the answers clockwise back in the WHEEL. The clues are not in the right order, and may overlap by one or more letters with the word in front or behind them. It's up to you to work out which is the right way to fill the WHEEL. The first letter of Answer 1 is in place, and we give you the length of each answer.

London station, where trains were bound for Portsmouth (8)

Devon seaside resort opened up through railways (7)

Former Russian ruler, replaced by Lenin (4)

Diplomatic dispute between countries (3)

Landing place in a port close to the water (8)

Sheds for servicing trains and locomotives (6)

Line that diverges then rejoins the main line (4)

Rail company or someone who used to connect phone calls (8)

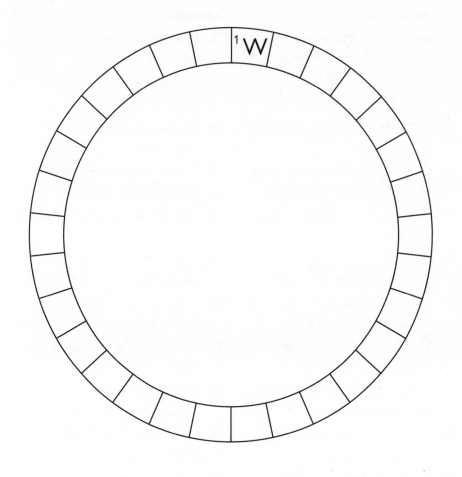

25. CRYPTIC

Get on board to answer these cryptic clues!

ACROSS

3 Build station, for example upright (5)

7 He provided Thirty-Nine Steps but not on foot – by rail (6)

8 Shift rota or speaker will appear (6)

10 Order right by her side at early rail Peak District route (10)

11 Change gear for French station (4)

12 Partly industrial railway in subcontinent (5)

13 and **18 Down**. Out east – and be quick about it! (3,6,7)

16 Ends red mix up at largest hauptbahnhof in Saxony (7)

21 Eurostar terminus for Walloons, linguistically (9)

22 Neil heads north to Bolshevik revolutionary (5)

23 Sounds like the travel fee for blondes? (4)

24 Add in with contents all over the world (10)

26 22 Across sees red here? (6)

27 Take out with mixed gin on short journey (6)

28 See 2 Down

DOWN

1 East unclear without a major Swiss hub (7)

2 and **28 Across**. Melancholy locomotive? (3,4,5)

3 Den's found where the line finishes (4)

4 Large book, like Bradshaw's, despatched to me (4)

5 Refreshment area before profit, it's a snip! (7)

6 Ring out the changes on the move (7)

9 Seen this gig which allows holidaymaker's indulgence (11)

14 No pen available to declare new railway ready to go! (4)

15 Laura loses a mix up to Asian mountain range (4)

17 Brake doesn't go down in fracture (5,2)

18 See 13 Across

19 Abandon wastelands overseas (7)

20 Far away land is tantamount to being in space it appears (7)

24 Lose the point at Ascot and provide warmth for guard (4)

25 Metal Mimi, Ron and I unearthed (4)

The Final Journey

The railways did not just carry the living! As railways allowed more people to travel in the nineteenth century, it also meant that more people started dying far away from home. In a time when the rituals of death bore such significance, it was imperative that the deceased were returned home to lie with their loved ones. Thus, the railway companies had special arrangements for the carrying of coffins. This included special hearse vans built for the purpose, as well as platform hearses to unload the coffins from the trains with dignity. Many famous people made their last journey by train, including Queen Victoria, Winston Churchill and King George VI. In the 1850s, London was so short of space to bury its growing population that the London Necropolis Railway was built to transport the deceased to a huge cemetery in Brookwood in Surrey.

26. THE ACCUMULATOR

Special agent, code name **Rocket**, has to find a left luggage locker at London's **King's Cross** station, which contains a secret message. He has been told that clues to the four-figure number of the locker will be revealed in a series of seemingly innocent station announcements. By the time you have finished the book you will have decoded the four clues and will have located the locker.

Here is the fourth and final of these clues. Which clue will **Rocket** pick up from this announcement?

> 'This train is very busy, and people are queuing. Please wait your turn in every queue and we will depart very soon.'

THE SOLUTIONS

Puzzle 1: **COGNITIVE**

C = clockwise. A = anti-clockwise

1 (C) Rivets; **2** (A) Arrive; **3** (A) Brakes; **4** (C) Ticket; **5** (C) Racing; **6** (A) Starts.

Puzzle 2: **STATIONGRAM**

The station is **EASTBOURNE**.

Puzzle 3: **A LONG DAY**

He finished his shift at **7.30 p.m**. The pickaxe work took up a quarter of the day, which equals 25 per cent of his time. The loading time was 35 per cent of the day. Add 25 per cent to 35 per cent to get 60 per cent. The digging took up five hours. As a percentage of his day that must be 40 per cent. If five hours equals 40 per cent, then one hour would equal 8 per cent of the day (40 ÷ 5 = 8). 8 per cent is multiplied by 12.5 to make 100 per cent. The navvy has worked 12 and a half hours. Starting at 7.00 a.m, he finishes at 7.30 p.m.

Puzzle 4: **A TO Z**

The words reading **ACROSS** from left to right, top to bottom are:

Derail; Operator; Area; Speed; Boat; Loads; Schedules; Express; Cafeteria; Joins; Link; Money; Turn; Changing; Equals.

The words reading **DOWN** from left to right, top to bottom are:

Tearooms; Hazards; Class; Bend; Harbour; Voyage; Excursion; East; Axle; Controls; Weekend; Contour; Alight; Tyres; Mail.

1 = S, 2 = P, 3 = E, 4 = D, 5 = I, 6 = A, 7 = R, 8 = L, 9 = X, 10 = M, 11 = O, 12 = C, 13 = G, 14 = T, 15 = H, 16 = Z, 17 = W, 18 = K, 19 = Y, 20 = J, 21 = B, 22 = F, 23 = N, 24 = Q, 25 = V, 26 = U.

Puzzle 5: **CHANGING STATIONS**

1 Blackburn, **2** Blackpool, **3** Lancaster. The ? sign stands for a letter **L**.

Puzzle 6: **PASS TIMES**

The train has travelled **30 miles** in total. The first journey is 16 miles (8 mile ascent plus 8 mile descent). The second journey is 8 miles (4 mile ascent plus 4 mile descent). The third journey is 4 miles (2 mile ascent plus 2 mile descent). The fourth and final journey is 2 miles (1 mile ascent plus 1 mile descent).

The total time spent travelling is **6 hours 15 minutes**. Ascent is 15 miles at 10 miles per hour = 150 minutes. Descent is 15 miles at 15 miles per hour = 225 minutes. 150 + 225 = 375 minutes.

Puzzle 7: **PUZZLE TRIP**

Mr Bright/Aviemore/Three/Logic.
Mrs Cross/Inverness/Four/Word fit.
Mr Down/Stirling/Five/Crosswords.
Ms Smart/Kingussie/Two/Word search.
Mr Winner/Gleneagles/One/Sudoku.

Puzzle 8: **MAKING TRACKS**

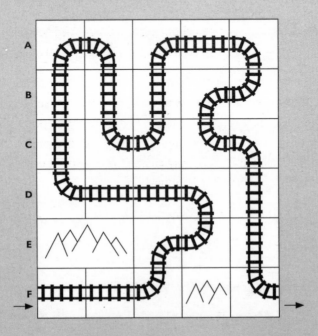

Puzzle 9: **LINE NINE**

TAY BRIDGE.

A) BARRIER; **B)** READY; **C)** GREAT.

Trivia Questions – Stations

1 London Waterloo – 86.9 million passengers in 2019/20.

2 Birmingham New Street – 46.5 million passengers in 2019/20.

3 They are all fictional stations (Llantisilly is from *Ivor the Engine*; Knapford is from *Thomas and Friends*; Felpersham is from *The Archers*; and Snettleford is from *Dad's Army*).

4 Abbey Wood.

5 Ystrad Rhondda (there are no stations starting with the letter Z).

6 Llanfairpwllgwyngyllgogerychwyrndrobwllllantysiliogogogoch – or Llanfair P G, as it is frequently shortened to. The name translates to 'the church of St Mary in the hollow of white hazel trees near the rapid whirlpool by St Tysilio's of the red cave'.

7 There are eleven stations to choose from: Ash, Ayr, Ely, IBM, Lee, Lye, Ore, Par, Rye, Wem and Wye. Pîl is also acceptable – it is the Welsh name for Pyle station.

8 Berney Arms near Yarmouth, with only forty-two passengers, although the station was only served for five weeks of the year due to line closures. It has no road access and mostly serves a local nature reserve. Britain's least used station usually changes every year because it attracts lots of enthusiasts after it is announced.

9 Scarborough station – it is 139 metres long.

Puzzle 10: **FROM A RAILWAY CARRIAGE**

The word that appears twice is **BRIDGES**.

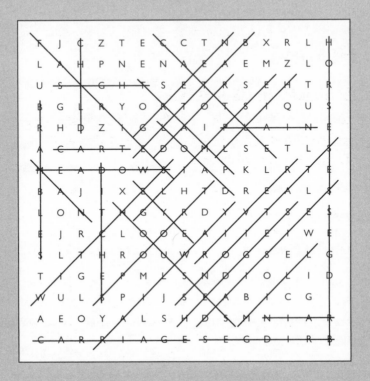

Puzzle 11: **RACK RAILWAYS**

1 Wales; **2** Switzerland; **3** India; **4** Brazil; **5** Italy; **6** Spain.

Puzzle 12: **STATIONGRAM**

The station is **ABERYSTWYTH**.

Puzzle 13: **MAP THE JOURNEY**

Journey **1 to 2**: Fort William to Glasgow is 123 miles.

Journey **3 to 4**: Dundee to Aberdeen is 58 miles.

Journey **5 to 6**: Swindon to Penzance is 191 miles.

Journey **7 to 8**: Skegness to Nottingham is 63 miles.

Puzzle 14: **WHERE AM I?**

TRURO.

The first letter could be **S** or **T**. The second letter could be **R**, **T** or **U**. The third letter is **U**. The fourth letter is **R**. The fifth letter is **O**. Truro is the only station that can be formed by these options.

Puzzle 15: **SLANGING MATCH**

1 Lord Lovel/Shovel; **2** Bark and growl/Trowel; **3** Sugar and honey/Money; **4** Frog and toad/Road; **5** Billy Gorman/Foreman; **6** Pig's ear/Beer; **7** Jimmy Skinner/Dinner; **8** Tiddly wink/Drink.

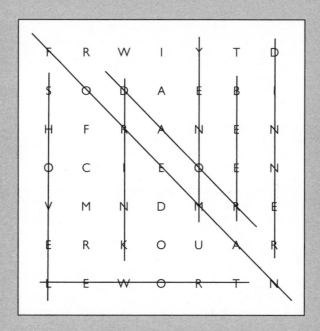

Puzzle 16: **QUOTABILITY**

1 Calendar; **2** Holidays; **3** Advanced; **4** Red light; **5** Labourer; **6** Emigrate; **7** Standard; **8** Day trips; **9** Inclines; **10** Corridor; **11** Keepsake; **12** Engineer; **13** Networks; **14** Stopping.

The author was **CHARLES DICKENS**, and the full quotation is: 'I am never sure of time or place upon a railroad. I can't read, I can't think, I can't sleep, I can only dream.'

Puzzle 17: **BRIDGES**

1 Long; **2** Field; **3** Hill; **4** Land; **5** Stream.

Puzzle 18: **POINTS**

The word is **FLAG**. It makes the words FLAGON, FLAGRANT and FLAGSHIP.

Puzzle 19: **SPLITS**

1 Build/Stone; **2** Peaks/Steep; **3** Canal/River; **4** Hills/Views; **5** Spades/Shovel

Puzzle 20: **THREE WAY**

1 Man; **2** Chest; **3** ER.

You are heading for **MANCHESTER**, one terminus of the Liverpool–Manchester Railway.

Puzzle 21: **HARD GRAFT**

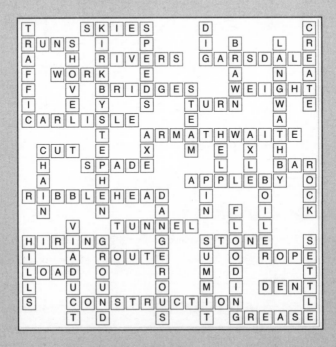

NAVVIES is the word that is left over.

Puzzle 22: **STATIONGRAM**

The station is **PETERHEAD**.

Puzzle 23: **THE RAILWAY CHILDREN**

There were just **THREE seats needed**. The grandmother was also a mother. Her daughter was also a mother. There was her daughter, who was also a granddaughter.

Puzzle 24: **WHEEL-RIGHT**

1 Forth; **2** Through; **3** Rough; **4** Heater; **5** Terrain; **6** India; **7** Diagram; **8** Met; **9** Turf.

Puzzle 25: **CRYPTIC**

ACROSS: **3** Staff; **7** Handle; **8** Apples; **10** Derailment; **11** Cars; **12** Track; **13** Spectator; **16** Catered; **21** Magazines; **22** Fares; **23** Flat; **24** Paddington; **26** Trains; **27** Enters; **28** Steam.

DOWN: **1** Careers; **2** Advance; **3** Sell; **4** Fast; **5** Special; **6** Leg room; **9** Temple Meads; **14** Crew; **15** Taxi; **17** *Mallard*; **18** Day trip; **19** Margate; **20** Detours; **24** Pass; **25** Item.

Puzzle 1: **COGNITIVE**

C = clockwise. A = anti-clockwise

1 (C) George; **2** (C) Rocket; **3** (A) Metals; **4** (C) Alerts; **5** (C) Stoked; **6** (A) Pledge.

Puzzle 2: **STATIONGRAM**

The station is **COLCHESTER**.

Puzzle 3: **SECTION SUM**

5 + 1 + 10 = 16

Puzzle 4: **A TO Z**

The words reading **ACROSS** from left to right, top to bottom are:

Resort; Fixtures; Zone; First; Flag; Times; Itinerary; Doorway; Fast train; Group; Crew; Begin; Maps; Overload; Outset.

The words reading **DOWN** from left to right, top to bottom are:

Velocity; Powered; Staff; Exit; Buffers; Repair; Returning; Near; Hour; Equipped; Steward; Promote; Arrive; Enjoy; Book.

1 = F, 2 = I, 3 = R, 4 = S, 5 = T, 6 = J, 7 = W, 8 = G, 9 = H, 10 = A, 11 = C, 12 = P, 13 = E, 14 = K, 15 = Z, 16 = M, 17 = X, 18 = N, 19 = B, 20 = O, 21 = D, 22 = Q, 23 = U, 24 = L, 25 = Y, 26 = V.

Puzzle 5: **CHANGING STATIONS**

1 Edinburgh, **2** Inverness, **3** Stranraer. The ? sign stands for a letter **R**.

Puzzle 6: **ROUTE FINDER**

There are **ELEVEN** different routes. All routes involve moving from A to B and finally D to E.

Variations on the route are:

1 B to C. C to D. A straight line heading south.

2 B to C due south. C to D taking the eastern loop.

3 B to C due south. C to D taking the western loop.

4 B to C taking the eastern loop. C to D due south.

5 B to C taking the western loop. C to D due south.

6 B to C taking the eastern loop. C to D taking the eastern loop.

7 B to C taking the western loop. C to D taking the western loop.

8 B to C taking the eastern loop. C to D taking the western loop.

9 B to C taking the western loop. C to D taking the eastern loop.

10 B to D taking the eastern loop and missing out station C.

11 B to D taking the western loop and missing out station C.

Puzzle 7: **AWAY DAYS**

Arnold/Cloudy/24 miles/Museums.
Brown/Thundery/56 miles/Shops.
Close/Rainy/30 miles/Theatre.
Dawson/Misty/10 miles/Friends.
Ewing/Sunny/48 miles/Gardens.

Puzzle 8: **RAILWAY READS**

1 *Murder on the Orient Express* (Agatha Christie); **2** *Strangers on a Train* (Patricia Highsmith); **3** *The Girl on the Train* (Paula Hawkins); **4** *The Thirty-Nine Steps* (John Buchan); **5** *The Mystery of the Blue Train* (Agatha Christie).

Puzzle 9: **LINE NINE**

PITLOCHRY.

A) CITY; **B)** PITCH; **C)** LORRY.

Puzzle 10: **SEASIDE SPECIALS**

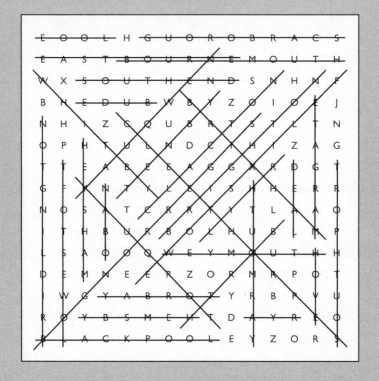

Puzzle 11: **CLOSURE**

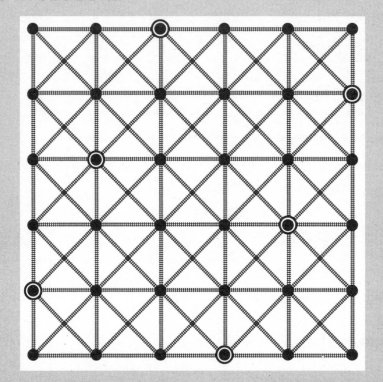

Puzzle 12: **STATIONGRAM**

The station is **WARRINGTON**.

Puzzle 13: **MAP THE JOURNEY**

Journey **1 to 2**: London to Hastings is 55 miles.

Journey **3 to 4**: Ipswich to Norwich is 40 miles.

Journey **5 to 6**: Douglas to Port Erin is 15.5 miles.

Journey **7 to 8**: Settle to Carlisle is 72 miles.

Puzzle 14: **WHERE AM I?**

CREWE.

The first letter could be **C** or **P**. The second letter could be **C** or **R**. The third letter is **E**. The fourth letter could be **R**, **T** or **W**. The fifth letter is **E**. Crewe is the only station that can be formed by these options.

Puzzle 15: **AVERAGE**

The average speed for the whole journey is **45 miles per hour**. Say, for example, the distance between places is 180 miles. At 90 miles per hour the trip would take 2 hours. The same route at 30 miles per hour would take 6 hours. That's a total mileage of 360, and a total time of 8 hours. 360 divided by 8 = 45.

Puzzle 16: **QUOTABILITY**

1 Gradient; **2** Whistles; **3** Enquires; **4** Nickname; **5** Distance; **6** Operator; **7** Lemonade; **8** Entrance; **9** Northern.

The character was **GWENDOLEN** (FAIRFAX), and the full quotation is: 'I never travel without my diary. One should always have something sensational to read on the train.'

Puzzle 17: **BRIDGES**

1 Ton; **2** Foot; **3** Band; **4** Board; **5** Time.
DARLINGTON is the proper name.

Puzzle 18: **POINTS**

The word is **ARCH**. It makes the words ARCHANGEL, ARCHBISHOP and ARCHWAYS.

Puzzle 19: **SPLITS**

1 Tours/Trips; **2** Queue/Seats; **3** Hotel/Sleep; **4** Aisles/Window; **5** Events/Launch.

Puzzle 20: **THREE WAY**

1 Pence; **2** ZA; **3** N.

You are heading for **PENZANCE**. Gilbert & Sullivan's operetta told the story of *The Pirates of Penzance*.

Puzzle 21: **DINING CAR**

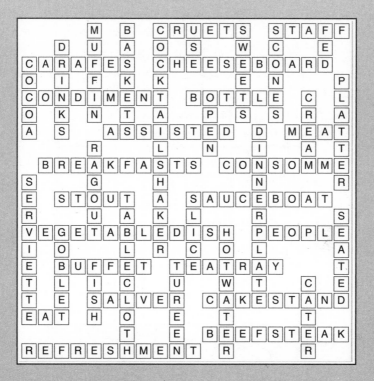

Puzzle 22: **STATIONGRAM**

The station is **BARNSTAPLE**.

Puzzle 23: **THE JEWEL IN THE CROWN**

The shaded squares reveal the number 6220, the number of the locomotive *Coronation*.

4	8	1	5	2	0	7	3	6
6	5	3	1	7	4	8	2	0
7	0	2	3	6	8	5	4	1
1	7	6	2	4	5	0	8	3
8	3	5	0	1	7	2	6	4
2	4	0	8	3	6	1	5	7
0	6	7	4	5	2	3	1	8
3	2	8	6	0	1	4	7	5
5	1	4	7	8	3	6	0	2

Puzzle 24: **WHEEL-RIGHT**

1 Velocity; **2** City; **3** York; **4** Kingdom; **5** Dome; **6** Merges; **7** Scottish; **8** Shovel.

Puzzle 25: **CRYPTIC**

ACROSS: **3** Tours; **7** Arrive; **8** Cotton; **10** Lime Street; **11** East; **12** Cheap; **13** Transport; **16** Non stop; **21** Platforms; **22** Axles; **23** Feat; **24** King's Cross; **26** Rejoin; **27** Custom; **28** Trunk.

DOWN: **1** Freight; **2** Fireman; **3** Test; **4** Scot; **5** Attempt; **6** Consort; **9** Refreshment; **14** Noon; **15** Soho; **17** Sleeper; **18** Station; **19** Express; **20** Tea shop; **24** Kent; **25** Sack.

Trivia Questions – Railway Jargon and Slang

1 B – the first signalmen were also policemen.

2 C – introduced in 1840 and used for 150 years.

3 C – tappers used hammers to tap the wheels and listen for signs of cracks.

4 A – a triangular shaped section of track, like doing a 3-point turn in a car.

5 C – first installed at Harrington station in 2008.

6 A – a slang term for a wheel chock.

7 A – the door through the streamlining used to access the smokebox for cleaning.

8 B – an experimental locomotive built for the Great Eastern Railway.

9 A – the valve prevents the build-up of a vacuum in a locomotive's cylinders when it is coasting.

Puzzle 1: **COGNITIVE**

C = clockwise. A = anti-clockwise

1 (C) Speeds; **2** (A) Needle; **3** (A) Tunnel; **4** (C) Turkey; **5** (C) Employ; **6** (C) Solves.

Puzzle 2: **STATIONGRAM**

The station is **MORECAMBE**.

Puzzle 3: **TUNNEL VISION**

The time taken is **5 minutes and 15 seconds**. The train has to travel the length of the tunnel plus its own length, which makes 5.25 miles in total. At 60 miles per hour the train travels a mile in a minute.

Puzzle 4: **A TO Z**

The words reading **ACROSS** from left to right, top to bottom are:

Porter; Trainmen; Jolt; Views; Away; Wagon; Squeaking; Sidings; Ownership; Trips; Fens; Visit; Iron; Elegance; Amazed.

The words reading **DOWN** from left to right, top to bottom are:

Monorail; Station; Drive; Cabs; Unpacks; Remain; Enquiries; Edge; Oils; Explored; Message; Arrival; Wheels; Steam; Vans.

1 = V, 2 = I, 3 = E, 4 = W, 5 = S, 6 = G, 7 = Q, 8 = C, 9 = J, 10 = Z, 11 = M, 12 = A, 13 = N, 14 = H, 15 = F, 16 = T, 17 = K, 18 = B, 19 = D, 20 = P, 21 = L, 22 = Y, 23 = R, 24 = U, 25 = O, 26 = X.

Puzzle 5: **CHANGING STATIONS**

1 Leicester, **2** Barcelona, **3** Santander. The ? sign stands for a letter **E**.

Puzzle 6: **NUMBER CRUNCHING**

MALLARD = 28.

DRAMA = 24, and no number can be greater than 6.

Therefore the letters must be represented by the numbers 3, 4, 5, 6, 6.

As A appears twice the value of that letter must 6.

As 3, 4, 5 and 6 are included in DRAMA, 1 and 2 must represent other letters.

That means I is either 1 or 2. L is either 1 or 2.

You now know that A + I + L will equal 9. From this the values of M, R and D can be fixed.

In DRILL the letters I, L, L must make a total of 5, so I must have a value of 1 and L must have a value of 2.

The letter values are: A=6; M=5; R=4; D=3; L=2; I=1.

Puzzle 7: **WIDENING HORIZONS**

Mr Driver/China/October/Flam Railway.
Mr Flag/Pakistan/April/West Highlands.
Mr Guard/Sudan/June/Harz Mountains.
Mr Porter/Australia/May/Douro Valley.
Mr Stoker/India/September/Albula.

Puzzle 8: **SHADED SEVEN**

1 Sunrise; **2** Midweek; **3** Jubilee; **4** Already; **5** Futures; **6** Interim; **7** Stamina.

The region is **SIBERIA**.

Trivia Questions – Railway Journeys

1 Leicester Square to Covent Garden, just 260 metres – a little over twice the length of the train.

2 Overnight sleeper trains.

3 1928.

4 They are all items of lost property left on trains.

5 Istanbul/Constantinople.

6 Australia – *The Ghan* which has forty-four carriages.

7 London and Paris – the train crossed the channel on a train ferry.

8 1980.

9 Penzance and Aberdeen.

Puzzle 9: **LINE NINE**

MAIDSTONE.

A) ESTIMATE; **B)** DONATE; **C)** DOMINATE.

Puzzle 10: **TRADING PLACES**

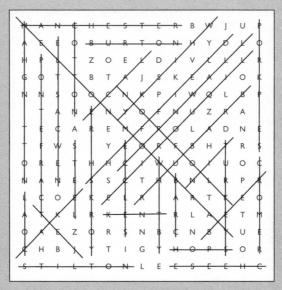

BURTON/BEER; CORNWALL/TIN; CROMER/CRAB; ECCLES/CAKE; KENT/HOPS; MANCHESTER/COTTON; MELTON MOWBRAY/PORK PIES; NEWCASTLE/COAL; NORFOLK/TURKEYS; NOTTINGHAM/LACE; OBAN/WHISKY; PONTEFRACT/LIQUORICE; SHEFFIELD/STEEL; STILTON/CHEESE; WHITBY/JET; YORKSHIRE/RHUBARB.

Puzzle 11: **SPEED TEST**

1 Speed; **2** Steep; **3** Tests; **4** Steam; **5** Dates; **6** Fastest.

Puzzle 12: **STATIONGRAM**

The station is **STONEHAVEN**.

Puzzle 13: **MAP THE JOURNEY**

Journey **1 to 2**: Caernarfon to Porthmadog is 25 miles.
Journey **3 to 4**: Scarborough to York is 36 miles.
Journey **5 to 6**: Durham to Newcastle is 13 miles.
Journey **7 to 8**: Bedford to Brighton is 91 miles.

Puzzle 14: **WHERE AM I?**

PERTH. The first letter is **P**. The second letter could be **A** or **E**. The third letter is **R**. The fourth letter is **T**. The fifth letter is **H**. Perth is the only station that can be formed by these options.

Puzzle 15: **AC/DC**

1 (DC) Corridor; **2** (AC) Cargo; **3** (AC) Change; **4** (DC) Conductor; **5** (DC) Record; **6** (AC) Coach.

Puzzle 16: **QUOTABILITY**

1 Barriers; **2** Rush hour; **3** Inventor; **4** Terminus; **5** Industry; **6** Schedule; **7** Historic; **8** Rapidity; **9** Accident; **10** Investor; **11** Landmark.

The company was **BRITISH RAIL**. The slogan was, 'Let the train take the strain.'

Puzzle 17: **BRIDGES**

1 Point; **2** Speed; **3** Staff; **4** Way; **5** Work.

Puzzle 18: **POINTS**

The word is **BAR**. It makes the words BARGAIN, BARRACK and BARROWS.

Puzzle 19: **SPLITS**

1 Start/Stops; **2** Danger/Hazard; **3** Record/Speeds; **4** Tested/Trials; **5** Success/Victory.

Puzzle 20: **THREE WAY**

1 Win; **2** Son; **3** D.

You are heading for **SWINDON**.

Puzzle 21: **LANDSCAPE**

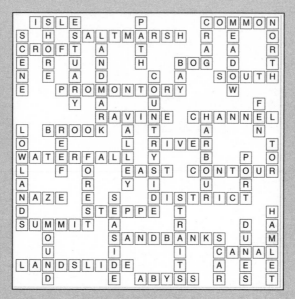

WEST is the word that is left over.

Puzzle 22: **STATIONGRAM**

The station is **HARROGATE**.

Puzzle 23: **ICEBREAKER**

1 Tickets; **2** Suitcase; **3** Noticeboard; **4** Pickaxe; **5** Service.

Puzzle 24: **WHEEL-RIGHT**

1 Streak; **2** Kremlin; **3** Lines; **4** Estuary; **5** Ryde; **6** Develop; **7** Points.

Puzzle 25: **CRYPTIC**

ACROSS: **3** China; **7** Tender; **8** London; **10** Metropolis; **11** Elba;
12 Coast; **13** Adventure; **16** Elevate; **21** Inverness; **22** Check; **23** Owns;
24 Prospector; **26** Hourly; **27** Argyll; **28** Stock.

DOWN: **1** Develop; **2** Address; **3** Crop; **4** Alps; **5** Invests; **6** Robbery;
9 Vladivostok; **14** Eats; **15** Glen; **17** Snowdon; **18** Leisure; **19** Chicago;
20 Schools; **24** Pays; **25** Peak.

Puzzle 1: **COGNITIVE**

C = clockwise. A = anti-clockwise

1 (C) Albert; **2** (A) Driver; **3** (A) Guards; **4** (C) Greets; **5** (C) Steers; **6** (A) States.

Puzzle 2: **STATIONGRAM**

The station is **GREAT YARMOUTH**.

Puzzle 3: **SECTION SUM**

200 + 5 + 15 = 220

Puzzle 4: **A TO Z**

The words reading **ACROSS** from left to right, top to bottom are:

Poster; Platform; Gaze; World; Pick; Ditch; Highlands; Quickly; Employers; Coach; Open; Vista; Rove; Levelled; Greets.

The words reading **DOWN** from left to right, top to bottom are:

Locality; Stretch; Crowd; Yard; Offpeak; Priced; Railcards; Hill; Busy; Excavate; Planned; Journey; Mapped; Cargo; Vale.

1 = W, 2 = O, 3 = R, 4 = L, 5 = D, 6 = H, 7 = E, 8 = N, 9 = I, 10 = U, 11 = K, 12 = A, 13 = P, 14 = C, 15 = S, 16 = F, 17 = J, 18 = V, 19 = X, 20 = M, 21 = T, 22 = G, 23 = Q, 24 = B, 25 = Z, 26 = Y.

Puzzle 5: **CHANGING STATIONS**

1 Volgograd, **2** Leningrad, **3** Astrakhan. The ? sign stands for a letter **A**.

Puzzle 6: **FROZEN TRACKS**

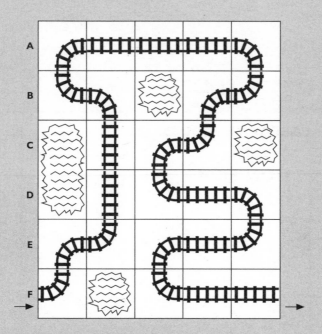

Puzzle 7: **END OF THE LINE**

Mr Bones/Eskmorn/Builder/Christie.

Mrs Case/Chilsale/Architect/Rankin.

Mr Cheatem/Brenton/Accountant/Rendell.

Miss Deeds/Durden/Tailor/Sayers.

Mr Ripper/Alesley/Lawyer/James.

Puzzle 8: **PLATFORM PUZZLE**

For Platform SIX he wrote 9.

For each platform number he extracted just the Roman numerals from the English spelling of the word. So for EIGHT he extracted the I as 1, for NINE he extracted the I as 1, for SEVEN he extracted the V as 5, and for FIVE he extracted the IV as 4. For SIX therefore he extracted IX, which are the Roman numerals for 9. Our Classics student never made it to the second day at the station.

Puzzle 9: **LINE NINE**

SINGAPORE.

A) PASSENGER; **B)** ENGINEER; **C)** ORGANISER.

Puzzle 10: **COMMUTERS**

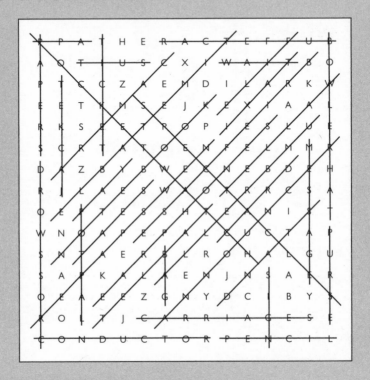

Puzzle 11: **KEY QUESTION**

The station is **TRURO**.

Puzzle 12: **STATIONGRAM**

The station is **CLEETHORPES**.

Puzzle 13: **MIX AND MILES**

Journey **1 to 6**: Amsterdam to Brussels is 108 miles.
Journey **2 to 8**: Copenhagen to Helsinki is 547 miles.
Journey **3 to 7**: Madrid to Lisbon is 312 miles.
Journey **4 to 5**: Vienna to Paris is 642 miles.

Puzzle 14: **WHERE AM I?**
RUGBY.

The first letter could be **A** or **R**. The second letter is **U**. The third letter is **G**. The fourth letter could be **B** or **G**. The fifth letter is **Y**. Rugby is the only station that can be formed by these options.

Puzzle 15: **ANNOUNCEMENTS**

1 Mind the gap; **2** There are leaves on the line; **3** Stand clear of the edge; **4** This service is delayed; **5** We apologise for the inconvenience.

Puzzle 16: **QUOTABILITY**

1 Stations; **2** Throttle; **3** Electric; **4** Platform; **5** Hedgerow; **6** Everyone; **7** National; **8** Starting; **9** Official; **10** Nineties.

The pioneer was **STEPHENSON** who said, 'One locomotive is worth fifty horses.'

Puzzle 17: **BRIDGES**

1 Ship; **2** Mouth; **3** Watch; **4** Class; **5** Alarm.
PORTSMOUTH is the proper name.

Puzzle 18: **POINTS**

The word is **PASS**. It makes the words PASSAGES, PASSPORT and PASSWORD.

Puzzle 19: **SPLITS**

1 Door/Link; **2** Pull/Cord; **3** Alarm/Brake; **4** Safety/Secure; **5** Access/Guards.

Puzzle 20: **THREE WAY**

1 Jee (sounds like the letter G); **2** Darling; **3** This is a famous tea growing area.

You are heading for **DARJEELING**.

Puzzle 21: **PLACE TO PLACE**

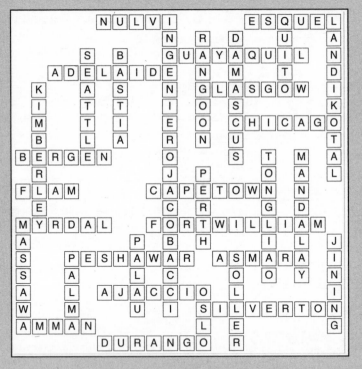

1/B; 2/D; 3/M; 4/P or Q; 5/O; 6/P or Q; 7/A; 8/L; 9/E; 10/C; 11/F; 12/I or J; 13/G; 14/I or J; 15/N; 16/K; 17/H.

Trivia Questions – Railway Bridges, Tunnels and Summits

1   The Tay Bridge in Scotland (although, if you are reading this after the opening of High Speed 2, the answer should now be the Colne Valley Viaduct, which will be slightly longer).

2   The Northern Line tunnel between East Finchley and Morden at 17.3 miles. The longest main-line tunnel is currently on High Speed 1 at 6 miles long, but the 10-mile Chiltern Tunnel on High Speed 2 will replace it once opened.

3   Hafod Eryri, or Snowdon Summit Station in Wales at 1085 metres above sea level on the Snowdon Mountain Railway. The remote Corrour station on the Scottish West Highland Line is the highest main-line station at 408 metres.

4   The Alps – the Gotthard Base Tunnel is 35 miles long, with a maximum depth of 2.45 kilometres.

5   Qinghai–Tibet railway between China and Tibet reaching 5072 metres above sea level.

6   The Royal Border Bridge is ironically the only railway structure on the list that does not cross a British national boundary. The Severn Tunnel and Chepstow Bridge both cross the England–Wales border. The Sark Viaduct crosses from England to Scotland at Gretna. The Royal Border Bridge is wholly within England at Berwick.

7   The Gaunless Bridge on the Stockton and Darlington Railway in 1825.

8   Ribblehead Viaduct on the Settle to Carlisle Railway – they were all temporary navvy settlements.

9   Twenty-four.

Puzzle 22: **STATIONGRAM**

The station is **WESTON-SUPER-MARE**.

Puzzle 23: **MURDER MOST FOUL**

The poisoner is **MAJOR ROUGH**.

Ivor Fortune gets on the train at Grimly Rise at 6.00 p.m. He is in carriage E.
Reverend Grey boards at Coldmoor at 6.20 p.m. He is in carriage A.
Major Rough boards at Wildfell Ridge at 7.00 p.m. He is in carriage D.
Sir Tom O'Hawk boards at Much Havoc at 7.10 p.m. He is in carriage B.
Lady Smith boards at Stormy Down at 7.20 p.m. She is in carriage C.
Miss Sparrow boards at Commonrow Hill at 7.40 p.m. She is in carriage F.

Puzzle 24: **WHEEL-RIGHT**

1 Waterloo; **2** Loop; **3** Operator; **4** Torquay; **5** Quayside; **6** Depots; **7** Tsar;
8 Row.

Puzzle 25: **CRYPTIC**

ACROSS: **3** Erect; **7** Buchan; **8** Orator; **10** Derbyshire; **11** Gare; **12** Indus; **13
and 18 Down** The Orient Express; **16** Dresden; **21** Bruxelles; **22** Lenin; **23**
Fair; **24** Continents; **26** Russia; **27** Outing; **28** See 2 Down.

DOWN: **1** Lucerne; **2 and 28 Across** The Blue Train; **3** Ends; **4** Tome;
5 Bargain; **6** Touring; **9** Sightseeing; **14** Open; **15** Ural; **17** Break up; **18** See 13
Across; **19** Deserts; **20** Distant; **24** Coat; **25** Iron.

Puzzle 26: **THE ACCUMULATOR**

In each section there is a hidden number in the announcement. The word is formed by joining parts of words together.

Section 1: 'This train will be delayed by a quarter of an hour. Some of our drivers have been taken ill.' The number FOUR is hidden.

Section 2: 'When the weather starts to freeze rooms are available, with heating, for you to wait in.' The number ZERO is hidden.

Section 3: 'Luggage must not be too heavy on this train. Does your luggage weigh too much? If so please alert the guard.' The number EIGHT is hidden.

Section 4: 'This train is very busy, and people are queuing. Please wait your turn in every queue and we will depart very soon.' The number NINE is hidden.

The secret locker number is **FOUR ZERO EIGHT NINE**.

RAILWAY **MUS**EUM

First opened in 1975 in York, the National Railway Museum
is home to many world-famous locomotives and an unrivalled
collection that celebrates the past, present and future of innovation
on the railways. Dedicated to igniting visitors' curiosity about the
people, places and engineering marvels behind the railways, the
museum's staff and volunteers put their passion for amazing stories
into everything they do.

NOTES

NOTES

NOTES

NOTES

NOTES

NOTES

If you've enjoyed travelling around Britain through these puzzles, make sure to check out the National Railway Museum's first puzzle book:

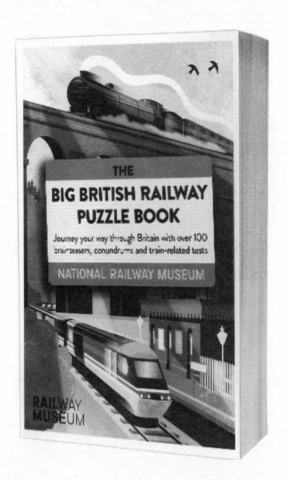